The Benevolent Bean

The Benevolent Bean

MARGARET & ANCEL KEYS

THE NOONDAY PRESS

A division of Farrar, Straus and Giroux, New York

We are indebted to many authors and publishers for permission to quote recipes, listed here alphabetically by author.

Beans and Bean Sprouts adapted from String Bean Casserole, from *Thoughts for Buffets* (anonymous). Reprinted by permission of Houghton Mifflin Company.

Bean Sprout Salad and String Beans with Shrimps, from *Hawaiian and Pacific Foods*, by Katherine Bazore. Copyright 1940, 1947 by Katherine Bazore. Reprinted by permission of William Morrow and Company, Inc.

Sicilian Seafood and Vegetable Salad adapted from Insalata Siciliana, from *The Southern Italian Cookbook*, by Colette Black. Copyright © 1963 by The Crowell-Collier Publishing Company. Reprinted by permission of The Macmillan Company.

Brazilian Black Beans (Feijoada) and Tutú of Black Beans, from *The Art of Brazilian Cookery*, by Dolores Botafogo. Copyright © 1960 by Dolores Botafogo. Reprinted by permission of Doubleday & Company, Inc.

Cassoulet de Castelnaudary, from *Bouquet de France*, by Samuel Chamberlain. Reprinted by permission of the author and Gourmet Distributing Corp.

Cassoulet de Porc et de Mouton, from *Mastering the Art of French Cooking*, Vol. I, by Julia Child, Simone Beck, and Louisette Bertholle. Copyright © 1961 by Alfred A. Knopf, Inc. Reprinted by permission of Alfred A. Knopf, Inc. and Cassell & Co. Ltd.

Spanish Cabbage, from *Mexico Through My Kitchen Window*, by Maria A. de Carbia, edited by Helen Corbitt. Reprinted by permission of Houghton Mifflin Company.

Cassoulet Ménagère, from *French Cooking for Americans*, by Louis Diat. Copyright 1941, 1946, by Louis Diat. Renewal, © 1969 by Mrs. Louis Diat. Reprinted by permission of J. B. Lippincott Company.

Cassoulet, from *The Escoffier Cook Book*, by A. Escoffier. Copyright 1941 by Crown Publishers, Inc., © renewed 1969. Used by permission of Crown Publishers, Inc.

Cassoulet, from *The Mistress Cook*, by Peter Gray. Copyright © 1956 by Oxford University Press, Inc. Reprinted by permission.

Cassoulet du Languedoc, from *La Cuisine et la Patisserie Française*, by Alfred Guérot, copyright © Flammarion Paris 1953. Reprinted by permission of the publisher.

PREFACE

Friends who learned that we were writing a book on bean cookery usually asked, "Why?" and added, "*Everyone* knows how to cook beans!" And that is the trouble: most cooks know a few recipes but have no idea of the variety of dishes they *could* prepare. Besides, we are concerned with all of the more common legumes—peas, lentils, chick-peas (garbanzos), peanuts, as well as the innumerable kinds of beans.

The distinctive feature of the *Leguminosae* is the ability of the plant to take nitrogen from the air and use it to build protein in the seeds. So beans and the like are high-protein foods, matching meat in this respect but with the difference that meat is high in fat, and the saturated kind to boot, in contrast to the leguminous seeds. Some species—soybeans, peanuts, and some lupines—produce seeds fairly high in fat, but the fat is the unsaturated kind that is favored by people who are worried about fats and cholesterol in the blood. Our interest in blood cholesterol and heart disease started us on the subject of beans. And then we learned that although almost everyone likes beans and their relatives, their cookery has been remarkably neglected; we searched in vain for a book on the subject.

Beans and the like lack the glamor of exotic, expensive foodstuffs. They are too cheap and universally available to get the attention and respect their flavor and nutritional excellence would otherwise command. The wrong kind of price-consciousness keeps them out of the kitchen of the pretentious cook and off the menu of the snobbish host. But people who reject conscious snobbery are apt to worry about status symbols and go out of their way to avoid whatever is locally abundant and therefore "common." We once spent a month in Cape Town before anyone served us lobster tails: "too cheap for company," they explained. No wonder, then, that in our part of the world people often hesitate to serve beans. "The poor man's meat" is an unfortunate label.

Someday we may write a book on food prejudices; the deterrent, besides our having other things to do, is our realization of how big a book might result. In the meantime, perhaps here we can make a dent in the prejudice about the Benevolent Bean. The title, incidentally, is derived from a quotation from Robert Smith Surtees, in *Handley Cross* (1843, Chapter 27) about the pleasant state of being "full o' beans and benevolence."

As is often the case with writing a book that seems to be a "natural," the job turned out to be more laborious—and more fun in this case—than expected. Among other complications, there are just too many kinds of edible leguminous seeds— over a thousand varieties of beans alone, according to one outdated estimate—and their classification is bewildering. Fortunately, though there are so many kinds, differing in color, shape, size, habit of growth, productivity, and horticultural preferences, for most cookery purposes it is enough to distinguish only a relatively few types. Each type has differing characteristics depending on the state of maturity and the processing it has received before it enters the home kitchen—fresh, dried, canned, frozen, partially or wholly precooked.

So there was much research to be done besides simply collecting, devising, and testing recipes. As for recipes, most of the more common stand-bys turned up in nearly identical versions in scores of cookbooks and were repeated in notes from friends about their "special family recipe," "Aunt Mary's invention," and the like. The true original sources of most bean recipes would be impossible to track down if, in fact, they ever had a single source. But even oft-repeated recipes needed testing to make sure of quantities, times, and the nuances of added flavorings. And testing for us means more than simply cooking and tasting the way it is done in the kitchens of some commercial food processors. We think that a sniff, a poke with the fork, and a bite or two are not enough to judge the real quality of a dish as a major part of a meal, even when several experienced food tasters pool their independent judgments. Testing each recipe our way requires eating a whole meal; a final selection of several hundred recipes means a lot of experimental meals.

Happily, we had much help, not only in eating the results but also in digging out the lore of the subject. Our youngest daughter, Martha, an enthusiastic bean eater, helped with the eating and appraisal in such time as could be spared from all the competing interests that engulf the teen-ager. Carrie, her older sister, sent recipes and shopping notes interspersed between news about the grandchildren. Henry, in medical school, and his wife Mollie, busy teaching and studying languages, were frequent helpful critics of our cookery monomania.

It is a pleasure to express thanks to Mrs. Nedra Foster and Mrs. Carol Thera for calculations of nutrient values and to Miss Carolyn Johnson and Mrs. Sandra Rondeau for typing. Dr. J. W. Hayward, formerly of Archer Daniels Midland Co., supplied information on soybeans. The list of people in many lands who supplied recipes and bean lore is too long to reproduce here, but we must mention Mrs. Maryel Gram and Mrs. Maud Joesting. To all of them we are grateful.

CONTENTS

Introduction

MEET THE BEANS AND
THEIR RELATIVES

A formal introduction to the bean and pea family is in order since there are so many relatives in the family of *Leguminosae*. We want you to meet *Phaseolus, Lens, Arachis, Pisum, Glycine,* and *Cicer*, better known to most people as beans, lentils, peanuts, peas, soybeans, and chick-peas. They all have much to offer when treated right.

Harsh things have been written about them. "Beanes are harde of digestion, and make troblesum dreames," William Turner wrote (1551) in his *Herbal*, and they do have the reputation of being "windy"; but this applies only to the dried mature seeds, which are now much improved in variety and processing. Besides, it is unlikely that the beans from the newly discovered Americas were known to Turner, and he almost certainly meant the broad bean which has little virtue in our opinion and is much more fibrous than the varieties commonly eaten today.

Beans have long been tagged "the poor man's meat." "Alwaie the bygger eateth the beane" (1562). The beggar in the Middle Ages, and long before then, took advantage of the high nutritional quality of beans which only lately has been demonstrated, by chemical analysis showing their high protein content and by biological experiments that prove their nutritional value. But a foodstuff popular among the poor was bound to be looked down on by the rich aristocrats and to be considered by them as a "second-class" food. A trial that refuted this snobbish idea was probably the first recorded dietary experiment on man. The story is told in the Book of Daniel in the Bible.

Nebuchadnezzar, king of Babylon, brought to his palace some children of the Israelites "in whom was no blemish but [who were] well favored and skillful in all wisdom." They were to be brought up as his subjects. "The king appointed them a daily provision of the king's meat, and of the wine which he drank." Daniel, one of the children, "purposed in his heart that he would not defile himself with the portion of the king's meat, nor the wine which he drank, therefore he requested of the prince of the eunuchs that he might not defile himself." The eunuchs were in charge of the children, and Daniel had found a friend in their prince, but the prince was afraid to change their diet lest they should look less well fed than the other children of the court. Daniel persuaded him to carry out a ten-day trial during which the diet for four of them would be only pulse (peas) and water. The prince was then to decide whether they seemed in better or worse health. "At the end of ten days their countenances appeared fairer and fatter in flesh than all the children which did eat the portion of the king's meat," and they were allowed to continue their diet of peas. And when the time came for them to be brought before King Nebuchadnezzar he found them not only superior in all learning and wisdom but "ten times better than all the magicians and astrologers that were in his realm" (Daniel 1:1–21).

Modern nutritional scientists are strong for a variety of foods in the diet because dominance of one foodstuff can lead to nutritional deficiency if that one foodstuff happens to be short of one or another vitamin or mineral. But peas are nutritionally remarkably complete, and it seems quite possible that the children of the Israelites could thrive on only peas and water, if, as is probable, they were often exposed to the strong sunlight of their part of the world. The sunlight would take care of the need for vitamin D.

Suppose Daniel's diet amounted to three thousand calories a day, with cooked fresh green peas providing an average of 15 per cent and dried peas the rest of the calories. His diet would have been well above recommended allowances in protein, thiamine, niacin, vitamin C, and iron; would have been sufficient in vitamin A, riboflavin, and essential fatty acids. Only calcium would have been marginal, but the hard water of that area would have provided more of that mineral.

There is no mention of complaints in the Book of Daniel about the monotony of the peas-and-water diet. Presumably, the people of those ancient days had simpler tastes. We once knew a medical scientist who calculated that one could live on a diet of hamburgers, and decided to make a test. Nutritionally, he got on very well for some weeks until the sheer monotony of only hamburgers three times a day put an end to the experiment. But there is no monotony in the recipes in this book.

TEN THOUSAND SPECIES

This book is concerned with recipes for the common beans and other legumes that are readily available in the United States and Europe, which means less than a dozen species. But the bean family, alias pea, mimosa, locust, etc., family or, better, the legumes or *Leguminosae*, includes over ten thousand species in close to five hundred genera. Most of these are of no direct interest for the kitchen, but the many important fodder plants in the family—the clovers, vetches, alfalfa, and some lupines—make a big indirect contribution. And our eyes feast on such ornamentals in the family as wisteria, broom, gorse, the locusts, laburnum, redbud, and the acacias in hundreds of varieties. Many lupines, as well as varieties of peas and beans, are prized for their handsome flowers.

The common feature of the leguminous plants is their ability to fix the nitrogen of the atmosphere by means of root tubercles and bacteria in the soil associated with them. Bacterial cultures can be bought to assure their presence for new plantings but this is unnecessary in most fields and gardens. The leguminous plants store up nitrogen, and proteins made from it, to the advantage of the bean eater and, when the plants are plowed back, to impoverished soils.

All of the plants in the family produce seeds made up of two valves, attached at the base to the inside of a pod; the term "legume" refers to this particular kind of seed growth. In some species the immature pods are favored for human consumption (snap beans and Chinese edible pea pods, for instance), but generally the seeds are much more important.

Probably most leguminous seeds would make good food if they were suitably prepared, but the preparation is complicated or tedious in some species. Soybeans are a case in point. Soybeans are edible but disappointing when the attempt is made to cook them like ordinary beans of the genus *Phaseolus*; yet Oriental populations long ago learned how to make excellent foods from them. A few methods are indicated in the chapter on SOYBEANS.

The seeds of some species of lupines make good food after lengthy preparation. The species *Lupinus tricolor* and *mutabilis* illustrate the kind of problem that vexes food experts who want to improve nutrition in areas where the diet is generally low in proteins. Those lupines are easily cultivated in mild climates and have no special requirements for soil or attention. The seeds have a high protein content, averaging over 40 per cent of the crude dry seed; flour made from these seeds averages about 56 per cent protein, 25 per cent fat, and only 14 per cent carbohydrate. As in most other leguminous seeds, the fat in the lupine seeds is relatively unsaturated.

These lupines grow well in the highlands of Ecuador at altitudes up to ten thousand feet but their cultivation and use is very limited because the local method of preparation of the seeds for human use is so cumbersome. Besides getting rid of tough skins, the problem is to remove bitter-tasting alkaloids. The natives cook the seeds in water for at least twelve hours and then wash them in running water for seven or eight days. This gets rid of the bitter taste—and also removes over 90 per cent of the water-soluble vitamins. The resulting product is much relished by the local populace; but if these lupine seeds are to contribute, as they should, to the correction of the general protein shortage of the region, more efficient methods of preparation must be developed. Lupine seeds and flour made from them are not found in any markets available to us, so we have not included recipes for their use.

STEP BY STEP TO
OUR INTEREST IN BEANS

Many years ago we took time out from responsibilities at Oxford University to work at the University of Naples. Envious colleagues suggested that we only wanted to exchange the cold and dark of English winter for the sunshine of southern Italy, but there was another reason. Neapolitans lived on a low-fat diet according to our friend Professor Gino Bergami of the University of Naples, so if our theory was correct, in that city we should find less coronary heart disease than in England, much less than in Minnesota, and the people should have low levels of cholesterol in the blood.

It was easy to check the truth of the low-fat character of the diet of the general population; at that time only 20 to 25 per cent of the dietary calories were provided by fats, while in England the figure was 35 per cent and in Minnesota it was about 40 per cent. And coronary heart disease was relatively rare except among a small upper crust of the population who ate a much richer diet. To check the blood-cholesterol story, men employed by the city of Naples were examined—clerks, firemen, and sanitary inspectors. Their cholesterol values were very low, averaging only 165 milligrams per 100 milliliters of blood serum, compared with averages in England over 200 and in Minnesota of about 230.

Perhaps these findings simply meant that the Neapolitans were different from Englishmen and Minnesotans in more ways than language and behavior. Still, a small sample of bankers and professional men in Naples, who lived on a much richer diet than the working class, had cholesterol values of about 200 in their blood serum and some of them had coronary heart disease. It would be impossible to carry out a controlled experiment to examine the whole story of diet fat, cholesterol, and heart disease, but at least experiments on the diet fat and cholesterol part of it could be done on men in Minnesota.

Carefully controlled experiments were made by our staff at the University of Minnesota and at one of the state hospitals. In a locked metabolic unit twenty-four physically healthy men were given, alternately, an ordinary American diet and a diet matching that of Naples in the percentage of fat, protein, and carbohydrate calories. Individual rations were adjusted to keep body weight constant. This meant equal amounts of protein (15 per cent of calories) but a contrast between 40 and 20 per cent fat calories, carbohydrate making up the rest of the calories. The results were clear-cut and in the expected direction: the average cholesterol value fell from 225 to 195 on the low-fat diet. But getting down to 195 was only halfway down to the Neapolitan figure of 165.

Actually a real Neapolitan diet was not used in Minnesota. Total fat, protein, and carbohydrate were matched, vitamins and minerals were adequate and similar, and calorie balance was maintained. But there were many differences in the foodstuffs. One difference between the low-fat diets in Naples and in the experiment was the character of the fat, which was chiefly olive oil in Naples and chiefly the fat in meat and milk in the low-fat diet fed in our hospital. These experiments coincided with dietary trials by our friend Dr. Lawrence Kinsell in California, which showed that when vegetable oils were substituted in equal amount for the common hard fats in the diet, the cholesterol level in the serum fell. This was long before the importance of the saturation of fat was understood, but it seemed probable that the difference between the kinds of fats in Naples and in our Minnesota experiment explained the discrepancy in the serum-cholesterol values.

Later controlled experiments in Minnesota and elsewhere brought order into the picture of the effects of different dietary fats on the blood cholesterol of man. So the data of the old Minnesota experiment on the bad imitation of the Neapolitan diet were recalculated. The difference in the kind of fat explained part of the discrepancy but not all of it. The Naples cholesterol values were still some 10 to 15 per cent lower than would be accounted for by the fats in the diet. Controlled experiments, with fatty acids as well as total fats being regulated, agreed; the cholesterol values in Naples were too low to conform with the theory of the time.

Even if our imitation Neapolitan diet had been "corrected" in the kinds of fats, it would not have been accepted as a Neapolitan diet in Naples. Where were the mountains of leafy vegetables, the abundant fruits, the beans and other leguminous seeds so prominent in the popular diet of Naples? New experiment more nearly matching the Neapolitan diet in these respects as well as in fats finally seemed to explain the serum-cholesterol discrepancy; there was no longer any reason to suggest that Minnesota men are basically different from Neapolitans.

But, as is usual in scientific research, there was a new problem to be solved. In the vegetables, beans, and fruits something must be affecting the cholesterol level, something not present in equal calories of bread and potatoes which generally take their place in the American diet. Various experiments ruled out proteins and vitamins as important in this connection, so attention was given to the carbohydrates which had been fairly well ignored, except as sources of calories, in past dietary studies.

The late Dr. Norman Jolliffe called ordinary carbohydrates "empty calories." But even the simplest carbohydrates—sugars and starches—are not all that simple; they all yield about four calories per gram (1816 calories per pound) but they differ chemically and in the way they are used by the body. However, in all ordinary amounts in the diet, the simple carbohydrates are much the same in their effect, or lack of effect, on the cholesterol in the blood. The blood-cholesterol picture was not explained by more potato starch, ordinary sugar, and lactose (milk sugar) in the American diet than in Naples, more wheat starch and glucose and fructose (in fruits) in the Neapolitan than in the American diet.

Complex carbohydrates might be something else. These non-sugar, nonstarch carbohydrates are very complex indeed, and except for cellulose (fiber or the equivalent of paper), which is indigestible by man, nutritionists have paid almost no attention to them. The diet contained a little more fiber in Naples than in the United States, but the total amount of fiber was small, perhaps a third of an ounce a day at most. Anyway, adding half an ounce of cellulose to the daily American diet had no effect at all on the blood cholesterol. Other laboratories confirmed our findings both with animals and with man. Cellulose or fiber gave no useful answer.

Another complex carbohydrate to think about is pectin, the substance that causes fruit juices to jell when they are boiled down with sugar. Pectin has many industrial uses including a small sale in the food industry. It used to be made from apples, but most of it in the market now is made from the peel and other waste left after making orange and grapefruit juice.

So pectin was tried, half an ounce daily, and this did have an effect. On the average, serum cholesterol went down about 5 per cent. This finding was also confirmed by others both in man and in experimental animals. Recently even as little as six grams daily (less than one fourth of an ounce) is reported to have a small effect on serum cholesterol. The Naples diet probably provides a little more pectin than the American diet but hardly enough to matter, and we still were not satisfied that everything was explained.

When menus were compared in detail, one item stood out: the difference in the amount of beans in the diets seemed worth further study. The American diet provided far fewer beans than in Naples; *pasta* and beans (*pasta e fagioli*) is a perennial favorite, especially among the common folk we studied most in

Italy. "Perennial" is a poor word to choose; *settimanale* (weekly) would be better. So more experiments were in order.

A good test would be to study a group of men in a metabolic ward of a hospital on a diet constant except for periods in which beans would replace equal calories of simple carbohydrate and, in parallel, another matched group of men who would make the reverse replacement, simple carbohydrate for beans. But if the beans did lower serum cholesterol we wanted to know what in the bean was responsible. Dried beans run about 21 per cent protein, 77 per cent carbohydrate, and 1 or 2 per cent fat. The fat would be too trivial to matter, but what about the protein?

There were some reasons for believing that the bean protein would have no special effect, but to rule out this possibility comparison was made of beans versus simple carbohydrate *and* pure bean protein equal to the amount in the beans. As it worked out, the diet averaged 3040 calories daily, with 124 grams of protein and 40 per cent fat calories (20 per cent saturated fat calories). The only difference was that in the bean period the men ate a daily average of nearly 200 grams (over six ounces) of a mixture of navy beans, lima beans, and split peas, while in the nonbean period, pure bean protein and simple carbohydrate provided the same calories and the same amount of bean protein as had been in the beans. Let us admit that this is overdoing it a bit; it was definitely a high-bean diet.

The result with twenty-four men was that serum cholesterol was about 9 per cent lower when the men were eating beans than when the beans were replaced by bean protein and simple carbohydrate. The experiment was repeated and the average difference was the same. The effect is not spectacular but it is not insignificant. And this effect of leguminous seeds in the diet was confirmed in Holland by an experiment on twenty volunteers, and in experiments on both rats and men in India. Brown beans were used in Holland and chick-peas in India. So if you happen to be interested in cholesterol control, beans, or any leguminous seeds, merit a prominent place in your diet.

THE TREND OF THE TIMES

Before we got so deep in the subject we had a vague notion that Americans used to eat more beans and their relatives than now. But we were wrong, at least in regard to the trend since 1909, when the U. S. Department of Agriculture first began to maintain detailed national records of "domestic disappearance" of foods for human consumption. Who eats what is not recorded; the per capita consumption is simply the total amount of food used in the year divided by the total population. In 1964 the per capita consumption was 7.5 pounds of dry beans and peas. For the five years from 1909 through 1913 the average was about 7.0 pounds. The peak use was at the start of rationing in World War II, when the per capita use was 11.7 pounds for the year 1942; otherwise the variations over fifty-five years have been small.

Americans are now eating peanuts at a yearly rate of around five pounds (shelled) per person; the figure has been climbing steadily for many years. So, if allowance is made for fresh, canned, and frozen peas, on a dry basis our total annual consumption of leguminous seeds is around fourteen pounds per person or about sixteen grams (a little over half an ounce) daily. This means only around 2.5 per cent of our total calories, so no one can say that Americans are fat from eating beans and peanuts.

When we tell people to eat more legumes they are apt to say, "What? Beans? But you can't eat a lot of beans!" Nonsense. Our experimental subjects ate 100 grams (over three ounces) a day for months and got along fine. In the district of Apulia in southern Italy dietary surveys showed an average per capita consumption of eighty-two grams of beans daily. And those people, though poor, get along fine too.

Perhaps it would be overdoing it to urge that everyone eat a pound of beans a week, but half a pound a week might be a good idea. That would double our intake of legumes and something else in the diet would have to be reduced to keep total calories in line. Our proposal would be to reduce sugar. Nutritionally, and gastronomically too, it is scandalous that Americans get some 16 per cent of their calories from sugar and other sweeteners. If we substituted twelve pounds of beans for an equal amount of sugar in the yearly diet, we would still be eating around eighty-five pounds of sugar a year.

PROTEINS IN LEGUMES

Authorities who are concerned with world nutrition say the biggest problem is protein, so they are enthusiastic about leguminous seeds because they provide more protein at less cost than from any other source. On the other hand, spokesmen for the meat and dairy industries point out that the protein in their products is "better" because it takes more bean protein than meat or milk protein in the diet for growth and maintenance of the body. They say that bean protein is of poor quality.

Protein quality is evaluated in various ways, most commonly by measuring the weight growth of young rats fed a diet containing the test protein. Or the absorption and retention by the rats of the dietary protein is estimated. With such experiments in which the test protein is the only protein in the diet, soybean protein turns out to have a little lower quality than beef muscle protein, but the protein of peas and ordinary beans may be only 60 per cent as good as the meat protein. This means that whatever the amount of meat protein would be the least needed, more than half again as much bean protein would be required. Cereal proteins, from wheat and rice, for example, are not much better in these tests.

But this is not a realistic approach: no one has only one kind of protein in the diet. A combination of bean and cereal protein is nearly as efficient as meat protein. Many populations the world over actually have developed smart answers to the protein problem in this way. Dishes of rice and beans, popular in Latin America and many other regions, provide high-quality protein at low cost. The same is true of the wheat and legume meals much used in Southern and Western Europe and in India; examples are beans and *pasta* in Italy, chick-peas and *chupatties* (like tortillas but made of wheat instead of corn flour) in India. The Japanese diet depends much on rice and *tofu*, a concentrate of soybean protein, and this combination is a highly efficient substitute for meat and milk.

FAT AND FATTY ACIDS

For people who want to cut down on fat in the diet, beans and their relatives are made to order. Except for soybeans, which are special, beans contain only from 1 to less than 2 per cent fat; not more than 4 per cent of the calories provided by ordinary beans are fat calories.

People who know about nutrition and possible relationships between the diet and the development of hardening of the arteries (the serious, atherosclerotic kind) and heart attacks talk as much about the kind of fat as they do about the total amount in the diet. The enthusiasts shudder at "saturated" fat (they really should say saturated fatty acids), and dwell lovingly on linoleic acid and the "poly-unsaturated" fatty acids in general. And in this respect what little fat there is in ordinary beans ranges from good to excellent.

The fat in beans and their allies is not only low in "saturates"; it is high in the essential fatty acid, linoleic acid and tends to be very high in linolenic acid. Next to that in linseed oil, the percentage of linolenic acid in bean fat is about the highest of any ordinary fat. Mention of linseed oil is hardly a good selling point if one recalls that the smell of the paint used on the outside of houses is that of linseed oil. But that unpleasant odor comes from chemical changes in linseed oil when it is exposed to the air for a few days.

In dried beans, and in flaxseed, the fat, including the linolenic acid, is stable in its natural environment, namely in the seeds that contain it. Immediately after linseed oil is extracted it is not disagreeable. It used to be the custom in some places in Central Europe to press the linseed oil out of flaxseed on Saturday afternoon and eat it on mashed potatoes for supper. The local lore had it that this use of linseed oil was good for the stomach. Though it was probably already pretty "ripe" by Sunday dinnertime, any of the oil left over was not wasted; it could be used to make paint.

Sven Hedin, the Swedish explorer, tells of the time he ran out of food while crossing the Gobi Desert. For unexplained reasons, the caravan happened to have a supply of linseed oil along so they fed some to the camels. Though the camels protested, they seemed none the worse. Then some of the men tried it but wished they had not.

LEGUMES IN THE DIET FOR HEALTH

As yet there is no proof that Americans would be protected against hardening of the arteries and heart attacks by lowering the blood-cholesterol level either by diet or by any other means. All that can be said is that substantially all doctors and informed members of the general public would rather have lower than higher cholesterol values in their own blood. Whether they are willing to change their diets on this account is another matter. Many people are skeptical or unwilling to make any effort. That is their business.

On the other hand, many people are asking for dietary advice with a view to blood-cholesterol control. We would not suggest trying to get 20 per cent of their dietary calories from beans and peas as did the experimental subjects described above. It is perfectly safe, as well as cheap, but it makes a lot of beans. But it is reasonable to get, say, 10 per cent of calories from leguminous seeds. And this will reduce the serum-cholesterol level a little—not enough to get excited about, perhaps, but this effect is in addition to any effects than can be produced by controlling dietary fats or other means.

SOME HISTORY

"Esau sold his birthright for a mess of pottage" is the chapter synopsis in an old translation of the Bible (the Genevan Bible, 1560). In the King James Version, the topic for Chapter 25 of Genesis states, "Esau sold his birthright" and in verse 34 we read, "Then Jacob gave Esau bread and pottage of lentils."

The preparation of lentil pottage, or soup, is depicted in a fresco of the time of Rameses III (1200 B.C.), but lentils were used in Egypt for at least a thousand years before then. Remains of lentils have been found in tombs of the Twelfth Dynasty (2400–2200 B.C.). And, though that seems to be a very long time ago, leguminous seeds go back to much earlier times.

There is evidence of the cultivation of legumes in the Neolithic period when man was passing from the hunting and food-gathering stage to the stage of food producing. This change did not take place at the same time in all parts of the world. Apparently in the Near East it occurred between the ninth and the fifth millennia B.C. as a result of the coexistence of wild plants and animals suited to domestication. With the radio-carbon method, archaeologists have dated remains of wheat, peas, and lentils found at Halicar, Turkey, at about 5500 B.C. Peas, lentils, and a legume called blue vetchling found at Jarno in Turkestan probably antedate the Halicar material by a thousand years. So legumes have been eaten by human beings for at least eight thousand years in that part of the world.

In North America legumes also go back many thousands of years. Remains of a legume not known in the Old World until the time of Columbus were found in caves in Ocampo, Mexico, and were dated by radio-carbon at about 4000 B.C. These were kidney or haricot beans, *Phaseolus vulgaris*, the species which also includes green and wax beans, navy and great northern beans, and the varicolored pinto beans—in fact, most of the varieties we think of as "beans" today. These were the beans that helped make possible the great voyages of exploration after the discovery of America; this nonperishable, rich source of protein nourished sailors all over the world's oceans for hundreds of years.

The kidney or haricot bean has been widely cultivated throughout North, Central, and South America since early times. The many varieties and names given to them by the American Indians are further evidence of antiquity. Vessels containing dried kidney beans have been found in pre-Inca tombs in Peru. One tomb, at Nasca in that country, contained jars decorated with figures of men or women holding corn (maize) in one hand and beans in the other. Another Peruvian jar, now in the Art Institute of Chicago, depicts a mythical battle of bean warriors, Mochica style.

Beans are mentioned by nearly all of the early explorers of the Americas. In 1492 Columbus found in Cuba a kind different from any then known in Europe, and later saw red and white varieties of the same bean in Honduras. Cartier (1535), Champlain (1605), Hudson (1609), and John Smith (1614) all mention local beans which undoubtedly were *Phaseolus vulgaris*. These beans, brought from America to Europe in the sixteenth century, at first were a rare luxury reaching only rich men's tables. Their easy cultivation and tolerance for a wide range of climates led to their extensive use all over the world.

LIMA BEANS

The lima bean was also a gift from the New World but it seems to have appeared later than the species *vulgaris*; at least the oldest remnants in pre-Inca tombs in Peru are dated only to about 1500 B.C. It is essentially tropical, or at least subtropical. In pre-Columbian times it was cultivated throughout tropical America, including Florida; now it is grown in many regions, including Africa south of the Sahara and in Southeast Asia. Its liking for the tropics is indicated by such names as the Burma bean, the Rangoon bean, and the Madagascar bean.

Two botanical groups are included under the name lima bean: *Phaseolus limensis,* in either the climbing or the bush variety, produces large flat seeds, while *Phaseolus lunatus* has smaller, rounder seeds and is often called the Sieva bean. Of two common commercial names, the Fordhook bean belongs to the former classification; the baby lima to the latter, while the term butter bean is used in some parts of the country to refer to either one.

Because the lima, or butter, bean will not grow in cool climates, until recently it was known to most of the world only in the dried form. The fresh, immature seeds had to wait for modern methods of processing and transportation before they could be made available to tables in the north. Lima beans are admirably adapted to the quick-freezing method, and their modern popularity is in the quick-frozen form.

The scarlet runner bean, *Phaseolus coccineus,* is another species of the genus *Phaseolus* that came from tropical America. In the mountains of Central America the dry, mature seeds are commonly eaten, but in other parts of the world only the immature pods and seeds are used and in the United States and Europe they are mostly cultivated for ornamental purposes.

Some other species of the genus *Phaseolus* also originated in the Americas but important species of the same genus are indigenous elsewhere. The mungo species, also called *Vigna mungo* or *Phaseolus aureus* or *Phaseolus radiatus* (we cannot decide about the differences of opinions of the botanists), seems to have originated in tropical Asia. Called mung, golden gram, green gram, black gram, and many other names according to the region and variety, this is one of the most important legumes in the tropics all over the world. The rice bean (*Phaseolus calcaratus*) also originated in tropical Asia and is widely grown in that part of the world. An important nontropical species is *Phaseolus angularis*, long grown and prized in Japan, Korea, Manchuria, and North China.

THE COMMON PEA

Together with lentils (*Lens esculenta*), noted above, the common pea has the longest history among the legumes we know today. *Pisum sativum* (also labeled *Pisum arvense*) apparently originated somewhere between India and the Mediterranean, possibly in the legendary Garden of Eden in the basin of the Euphrates and Tigris rivers. Remains of cultivated peas have been found in very ancient ruins in the Near East, in predynastic Egyptian tombs, in a neolithic village in Switzerland dated at about 4500 B.C., as well as in many more recent archaeological sites, including the city of Troy. It is safe to say that they have been cultivated for some eight thousand years. They were staple food in the classical period of Greece and Rome.

There are unmistakable records of garden peas in some of the writings of the old Greeks, but in most ancient writings there was no careful distinction among peas, beans, lupines, vetches, chick-peas, and lentils, so there is a vast field for conjecture. Theophrastus, who died in 287 B.C., made a clear differentiation in his *Enquiry into Plants* between *orobos*, vetch; *erebinthos*, chick-pea; and *pisos*, common pea. The Greek *pisos* became the Latin *pisum*, and *peason*, *pease*, and twelve other spellings in English. Theophrastus wrote of the pea as though it had been long well known, although the climate of the southern Mediterranean is a little too warm for the best cultivation of peas. Every early garden or agricultural book from Middle or Northern Europe includes discussions of the pea. It was much used in the Dark and Middle Ages, then became somewhat less popular after the introduction of beans and potatoes from America.

In J. Thorald Rogers' *History of Agriculture and Prices in England* we read: "Peas are frequently mentioned in the 'Expenses of Collegiate and Monastic Houses' in the years 1403–

1538. In those two centuries peas were so common that 'pottage' and 'porridge' meant peas." John Evelyn, the English diarist, in *The Compleat Gardener* (1693) lists peas as "great ones, little ones, white ones or yellow ones, and green ones." But fresh "green ones," in addition to the customary dried peas, were not common even as late as 1700, and apparently became popular in England only after a remarkable craze for them at the court of Louis XIV in France.

Judging from the cookbook of Apicius, the ancient Romans used dried peas; we find no recipe that would suggest the use of fresh peas. Or perhaps cooking fresh peas is too simple to merit a recipe from Apicius. At any rate, we doubt that the old Romans knew anything like the modern Italian fresh *piselli*. Between ourselves, we call them "unborn" peas and admire their tiny, greenish gold perfection of appearance. But the most luxurious *piselli* are too sweet and soft for our enjoyment more than a few times during their short season in Italy.

The consumption of peas increased explosively with the development of commercial canning which made nondried peas, formerly a short-season crop, available all year round. But few vegetables suffer more in the can, especially in Britain—where mint flavor, a bit of sugar, and artificial coloring contrive to make an even worse product than the usual American version. Frozen peas are a vast improvement, but the result of blanching and the addition of sugar is a product far inferior to real fresh peas. Happily, good, though often too mature, fresh peas now have a long season in the American market.

THE BROAD BEAN

The broad bean (*Vicia faba*), also appropriately called the horse bean, probably originated in North Africa but spread to many parts of Europe thousands of years ago. One variety has been found in Switzerland in deposits dating to the Bronze Age. Although grown in ancient Egypt, it was regarded as an unworthy food and does not appear in tombs or frescoes; the priests would not eat it. The ancient Greeks and Romans also held it in low esteem, as various anecdotes in classical literature attest.

Still the broad bean grows on an imposing plant, hardy and easy of culture, and it spread to all parts of the world. Early explorers brought it to the Americas—which is like bringing exceedingly poor coals to Newcastle. It is still rather extensively cultivated in Britain, where old ways cling more than in most places.

The Chick-Pea

The chick-pea (*Cicer arietinum*) was also cultivated from very early times in Mesopotamia and in the lands bordering the eastern Mediterranean, later spreading to India and other parts of Asia. It is not in the same botanical group as the common pea and resembles it only in being an edible leguminous seed. Chick-peas are called ceci in Italy, garbanzos in Spanish-speaking countries, and Bengal gram in India; they are eaten in great quantities in the warm countries where they are grown. They are almost unknown to many northerners but lately have become widely available in a ready-to-eat canned form.

The Peanut

The original inhabitants of the warmer parts of the Americas discovered and domesticated, for the ultimate benefit of the whole world, another legume of great importance today, the peanut (*Arachis hypogaea*, or *Arachides*), which the English call the ground nut. This is also called by many other names —monkey nut, *cacahuete* (in Mexico and Spain, from the Aztec), cacahouette (in France) *anchic* (in Peru), and *mani* (in most of Latin America). The early English name earth almond is now obsolete but an early American name, goober or goober pea, is still widely used in the southern United States. The names grass nut and pindar also refer to the peanut.

The Spanish conquistadors reported that peanuts (*mani*) were cultivated in Mexico, Central and South America, and the Caribbean islands. Early in the sixteenth century the Portuguese introduced peanuts into Africa, where they spread so rapidly that travelers a hundred years later thought they were indigenous there. During the same period peanuts reached the East

Indies, probably by way of the regular trade route between Mexico and the Philippine Islands controlled by the Spaniards.

In North America peanuts were not an important crop until late in the nineteenth century, though Thomas Jefferson mentioned their cultivation in 1792. In the twentieth century peanuts are produced on a large scale as an oil-yielding crop in the Americas, India, China, and Africa; the annual world production is over ten million tons, most of it as a source of oil for human consumption. Peanuts themselves are eaten in many countries though usually only in small amount. In the United States the consumption of peanuts as such has steadily increased from a little over 100,000 tons in 1910 to almost five times that figure in 1964. In most parts of the country peanuts are eaten only roasted, salted, in candies, and in peanut butter, but in the South they are frequently served boiled.

SOYBEANS

From China came another legume, the soybean. It is not known when it was first cultivated, but the earliest written record is found in books of the Emperor Shen Nung, dated 2800 B.C., which described the five principal crops of China; rice, soybean, wheat, barley, and millet. Later in that millennium there were writings giving expert advice on growing the soybean. It spread to Japan and other countries of East Asia.

The high protein and fat content of the soybean undoubtedly have influenced its history. The ancient Chinese evolved methods of preparing curd, cheese, sauces, and paste from the soybean which were used to flavor and enrich their staple diet of cereals. They also ate the bean sprouts as a vegetable. Such methods of using the soybean were described in Chinese writings at about the time of Julius Caesar.

In the earlier Chinese literature there is no mention of the soybean as a source of oil. However, some evidence exists that methods of expressing the oil were developed about the fourth century A.D. In Japan, Thailand, and Indonesia the traditional ways of preparing soybeans are similar to those of China.

Since the soybean not only is rich in protein and other nutrients, but is also a high-yield crop, the idea of encouraging its production and consumption in India, Africa, and other areas in which malnutrition is prevalent has appealed to many. In general, attempts to introduce it have not been very successful, chiefly because enthusiastic promoters of this legume have rarely realized that in its home in East Asia it is not prepared and eaten in the same ways as the common legumes elsewhere in the world, and the Orientals' elaborate processing is not easily introduced into other cultures.

The soybean, first brought to Europe from Japan in 1712 by a German botanist, Egelbert Kalmpfer, was grown as a curiosity in some European botanical gardens, including Kew Gardens in England, in the eighteenth century. Its first appearance in the United States was in 1804. Fifty years later Commodore Perry brought two varieties from Japan, but only in the first decade of the present century did it become an important export from Asia, first mainly to Europe and somewhat later to the United States. Its principal use in the importing countries was as a source of oil for soap-making and other purposes, and for the manufacture of livestock feed. Within the last thirty years the soybean has become an important crop in the United States not only for domestic use but also for export, with production close to 900 million bushels. This produces around 2.6 million tons of oil, of which nearly half is exported. Soybean oil meal, for animal feed, is being produced at an annual rate of around thirteen million tons in the United States, with over 20 per cent being sold abroad. Soybean protein preparations for human food, now being developed with much success, promise to be important in the diet of the future. These are discussed in the chapter on SOYBEANS.

DANGEROUS LEGUMES

Two diseases associated with the eating of certain legumes should be mentioned. One disorder, lathyrism, results from the contamination of wheat by a small hardy vetch called the lathyrus pea (*Lathyrus sativus*). In the Bible a familiar verse (St.

Matthew 13:25) says: "But while men slept, his enemy came and sowed tares among the wheat," which would seem to be an early form of biochemical warfare if the tares were *Lathyrus sativus*. Wheat contaminated by lathyrus or the lathyrus seeds themselves, if eaten in large quantities over a period of several months, can cause the disease, lathyrism, characterized by a spastic paralysis of the lower limbs. The disease, known since the time of Hippocrates, has occurred during recent centuries in France, Spain, Syria, Russia, and other countries, but it is particularly associated with India, where there were serious outbreaks as recently as 1944 and 1961. The neurotoxin which causes the paralysis has not been identified. There seems to be no risk of lathyrism when *Lathyrus sativus* seeds are eaten in relatively small quantities. Outbreaks of the disease are the result of semi-famine conditions which deprive people of their accustomed cereal and force them to rely too heavily on lathyrus.

Favism is an acute disease that develops in certain sensitive individuals shortly after eating broad beans (*Vicia faba*) or inhaling the pollen of the flower. The disease is almost entirely confined to persons living in the Mediterranean basin, or of Mediterranean origin. It is said to be particularly common in Calabria, in southern Italy, and in Sardinia. There is evidence that the victims have an inherited biochemical abnormality in the blood.

The Greek philosopher Pythagoras, who lived in the sixth century B.C., forbade his disciples to eat beans, and had such a horror of them that he would not walk through fields in which they were growing. This stringent prohibition was a mystery to Pythagorians in later centuries who tried to rationalize it in various ways. The most likely explanation is that Pythagoras suffered from the hereditary disorder which makes for sensitivity to favism, and had experienced one or more sharp attacks of the disease in early life. He met his death at the hands of the people of Crotona in ancient Bruttium (Calabria); pursued by them, he came to the edge of a bean field and rather than set foot in it he allowed himself to be overtaken and killed.

BEAN LORE AND LEGENDS

Things important in daily life over the centuries are bound to appear in stories and popular expressions. The age and importance of such items can be gauged, perhaps, by the frequency with which they turn up in songs and legends, and later in literature.

Among American Indians beans and corn are found together in many stories, as they were also often cooked together and grown together in the fields. There is a delightful story in Indian legend of the cornstalk as a young man, with his green-bladed robes shining in the sun and his tassels tossing in the breeze, who sang of his loneliness and his desire for a wife. The first to answer his song was a lovely vine with luscious green robes decorated with large yellow bell-shaped flowers, the young pumpkin or squash maiden. But the handsome young corn plant reluctantly turned her down because she wandered over the ground too much and he could not go with her. Then came the slender bean, her mantle spotted with flowers, who entwined her tendrils around the cornstalk and promised to love him forever, and this is the reason that ever since the bean twines closely around the corn and he supports her with his sturdy stalk.

The Indian custom of planting the beans in the same hill with the corn was commented on by many early explorers to the Americas. Van der Donck wrote, in 1656, of the Onondagas,

"They have a peculiar way of planting them [the beans of various colors and forms] which our people have learned to practice: When . . . maize is half a foot above the ground, they plant the beans around it and let them grow together. The coarse stalk serves as a bean-prop, and the beans run upon it."

One Indian legend records the origin of the bean and corn, according to Roger Williams (1643), as follows: "The crowe brought them at first an Indian graine of corne in one eare, and an Indian or French beane in another, from the great God Kautantowit's field in the southwest, from whence, they hold, come all their corne and beanes."

From the Grimms' story of *The Straw, the Coal and the Bean* we learn how the bean got her black stripe. She laughed so hard at the antics of the burning coal and straw as they fell into the river that she split. A tailor happened by and sewed her up. Ever since then the bean has had a black stripe because the kindly tailor used black thread for the stitching.

The prodigious growth of the broad bean inspired one of the best-loved fairy tales. The broad bean plant rapidly grows to twice the height of a child, so why not imagine a super bean-stalk and a small boy climbing up it to find a fabulous castle and a fierce giant at the top? Perhaps Jack lived in Leicestershire which "yieldeth great abundance of peas and beans, insomuch that there is an old by-word—Leicestershire Bean-belly" (E. Leight, 1659).

The ancient Greeks and Romans made use of beans in gathering the votes of the people. A white bean signified absolution and a black one condemnation. Surely this must have been the origin of the British custom of using white and black balls to represent votes for or against a candidate for membership in a club or other association. The rules provide that a stated proportion of "blackballs" shall exclude candidates proposed for election, and the candidate so excluded is said to have been "blackballed."

The bean has another election duty; it is traditionally put in the cake for the Twelfth Night celebration in England. The lucky man who finds the bean in his piece of cake is the master of the revelry. In fact, as Bean King he originally reigned for the twelve days from Christmas to Twelfth Night; his chief duty was the performance of magical ceremonies for ensuring good weather for the coming year. But now he is not chosen until Twelfth Night, and common British opinion is that the weather gets worse every year.

In another version, both a bean and a pea are put into the Twelfth Night cake; the man who finds the bean is king and the girl who finds the pea is queen of the festivities. If the bean is found by a girl, she may choose the king, and if the pea is found by a man, he names the queen.

In Italy today the bean plays a different role during the holidays. On New Year's Day it is traditional to eat lentils to bring wealth in the coming year; the more one eats, the more money he will have. In Texas, beans are the New Year's Day food to bring health, wealth, and happiness in the coming year.

In May there is cause for rejoicing, according to *Poor Humphrey's Calendar,*

> This month mackarel comes in season;
> And also reckon upon peason.

If you have experienced unpaved roads in spring, J. T. Hewlett's comment in *Parish Clerk* will describe for you the consistency of what we call pease pudding—"The roads were better, and not so much like peas-pudding."

It is more pleasant to contemplate William Butler Yeats's *The Lake Isle of Innisfree:*

> I will arise and go now, and go to Innisfree
> And a small cabin build there, of clay and wattles made
> Nine bean-rows will I have there, a hive for the honey bee
> And live alone in the bee-loud glade.

or perhaps to sympathize with:

> . . . an old person of Dean
> Who dined on one pea and one bean
> For he said, "More than that
> Would make me too fat."
> That cautious old person of Dean.

"Full of beans" is an expression used to describe a person full of energy and in high spirits, but when he is without money he "hasn't got a bean." He may be tall and lanky, a "bean pole"; perhaps he wears a "beanie." He will not be surprised if a friend greets him as "old bean," but he would hate to be spoken of as "not worth a bean" or "he doesn't amount to a hill of beans." To say that he "doesn't know beans" is to say that he doesn't know very much, but to say he is "beany" is to call him crazy. "Beano" is a treat or spree, but a "beanery" is a simple, unpretentious restaurant, while "bean house" is the foreman's office at a logging camp. There is even a verb "to bean" meaning to hit over the head or to hit with a bean from a bean blower or peashooter.

From the fourteenth century, "Lete hem ete . . . benes and bren ybaken togideres" suggests a method of preparing beans long since forgotten. The American Indians are also reported to have put beans in their corn bread.

Two centuries later Thomas Tusser wrote:

> Good peason and leekes, to make poredge in Lent
> And peascods in July, save fish to be spent.
> Those having, with other things, plentifull then
> Thou winnest the love of the labouring men.

"Poredge of peason" or pease pudding, was made by tying dried peas, which had been soaked overnight, in a cloth and suspending in a kettle in which the pork was simmering in a sufficient amount of water to cover both. When both were done, after cooking for about two hours, the pork was lifted out and sliced. The ball of peas was lifted out of its cloth onto a hot plate, and two forks back to back forced into the middle of the pudding thus pulled it apart. It should then fall into crumbly lumps. The hot pork broth was spooned over the pudding, which was then seasoned with pepper and served with the meat.

The "peascod" of Tusser's verse is an early word for "pea pod." We were amused to discover this old rhyme:

> Were women as little as they are good,
> A peascod would make them a gown and hood.

The pease pudding of old England turned up in New England as bean porridge, and we have seen the nursery rhyme written "Bean porridge hot" as well as:

> Pease porridge hot
> Pease porridge cold
> Pease porridge in the pot
> Nine days old.

Mrs. C. M. Poor contributed this discussion of bean porridge to *Mrs. Lincoln's Boston Cook Book* (1893):

BEAN PORRIDGE

This old-fashioned and very nutritious dish was one of the chief articles of winter food at my grandmother's farm in northern New Hampshire eighty years ago. When cooked, it was poured into bowls or basins holding from a pint to two quarts. A nice tow string was laid in a loop over the edge, and the porridge was placed where it would freeze. By holding the dish in hot water it would cause the porridge to slip out; then it was hung up by the loops in the "buttery," and was considered "best when nine days old." At early dawn the "men folks" who went into the forest "chopping" would take the skillet or a little three-legged iron kettle, and some large slices of "rye and Indian" bread in their pockets to keep it from freezing. The porridge was hung, wrapped in a clean towel, upon the sled stakes. Their spoons were made of wood. When it was twelve o'clock "by the sun," they kindled a fire with the aid of a "tinder box," warmed their porridge, and with their brown bread enjoyed this strong food as no modern epicure can his costly French dishes.

5 pounds corned beef, not too salty	*4 tablespoons cornmeal*
	Pepper and salt to taste
1 pint dry white beans	*1 pint hulled corn*

Soak the beans overnight. In the morning parboil in fresh water till soft. Put the corned beef in cold water, skim carefully, and simmer 4 to 5 hours, or till tender. Take out and cut into 2-inch pieces, and remove the bone and gristle; also the fat from the liquor. Put the meat and beans into the meat liquor, and simmer very slowly 3 or 4 hours, or till most of the beans are broken. Half an hour before serving, stir in the meal, first wetting it in cold water to a smooth paste. The meal should thicken the porridge to about the consistency of a thick soup. The meat should be cooked until it falls apart. Season to taste with salt and pepper. Add the hulled corn, and when hot, serve with brown bread. Sometimes potatoes, carrots, turnips or other vegetables frequently served with a boiled dinner are cooked with the meat, then removed, and the beans cooked as above, in the meat liquor.

Another early American recipe gives similar directions, but the list of ingredients does not include the hulled corn.

An age-old bean preparation from the Orient lends itself to easy reproduction in the home kitchen—the growing of sprouts from soy or mung beans.

HOW TO GROW BEAN SPROUTS

The basic method involves, first, soaking the beans overnight, then keeping them moist but not flooded in a warm (about 70° F.) dark place for 3 to 4 days, rinsing with fresh lukewarm water once or twice a day.

Various means are suggested to keep the beans moist. We have used all of the following with both mung and soybeans with equal success, placing the containers in a kitchen cupboard for darkness and even temperature: arrange a layer of beans in the bottom of a glass or pottery dish with a fitting cover; or place the beans in a wide-mouth jar, fasten cheese cloth over the top with a rubber band, prop the jar at a 45° angle with the mouth down in a dish containing a half-inch of water; or spread the beans between folds of cloth in plastic bags or any covered container. When the sprouts are about 2 inches long, detach them from the beans and store in the refrigerator. Consult the index for suggested uses.

Recipes

RECIPES

The recipes are arranged in the following sections: SOUPS, BEAN POTS, CASSOULET—BEAN STEW IN THE GRAND MANNER, LUNCH OR SUPPER, DINNER, VEGETABLES, SALADS, SOYBEANS and BEAN COOKERY IN IMPERIAL ROME. Recipes are included for peas, lentils, peanuts, chick-peas, and soybeans as well as the members of the *Phaseolus* branch of the *Leguminosae* family, whom you met in the INTRODUCTION. Many beans familiar to us all belong to that group, among them green beans (also called snap, string, stringless, and pole), wax beans, lima or butter beans, and the large variety of dried white, red, brown, black, pink, and spotted beans.

Since dried beans are universally available in all seasons, they hold a prominent place in this cookbook, and a few general remarks concerning their preparation here will save repetition in the recipes in which they are used.

In the following section, as elsewhere, the nutrients in each recipe have been calculated from tables of food composition and are given in abbreviated form: "cal." for calories, protein and fat given in "g." (grams), with grams of saturated fat expressed as "sat." and grams of poly-unsaturated fat as "poly." The word calories, wherever used in this book, refers to kilocalories.

Cooking dried beans is usually a three-part procedure; soaking, simmering, and, finally, combining with other ingredients for flavor and variety. The soaking can be shortened or even omitted by lengthening the simmering time. The third procedure can be anything from a quick reheating with other ingredients to slow baking together for hours. But the soaking, simmering, and slow baking require almost no attention from the cook, so she will not find herself "standing over a hot stove all day." Canned and precooked dried beans, ready for the third part of the cooking process, are plentiful. They are much more expensive than dried beans but are welcomed by cooks with a short meal-preparation time or who cater to only one or two people.

The method of preparing dried beans varies from country to country and cook to cook mainly in the quantity of water used. At one extreme the beans are put to soak in a large quantity of water, which is then discarded and replaced with fresh water in which the beans are boiled. This is also discarded, and a third liquid, often water, added with the other ingredients for the final phase of the preparation. At the other extreme are the cooks who warn against too much water for soaking, and who boil the beans in this same water, cooking until it has been almost completely absorbed or evaporated.

No useful purpose is achieved by large quantities of soaking or cooking water which are thrown away—on the contrary, valuable nutrients and flavor are lost that way. Except in the case of soup, it is best to use only enough water to prevent burning and to ensure tender beans.

SOUPS

Probably the most obvious, the most nourishing, the most universal and standardized use of dried beans is in soup. The beans are usually soaked overnight, then simmered slowly with the addition of other vegetables, and often a ham bone or bits of ham or bacon. Nearly all such soups include onion, celery, and carrot and are seasoned with garlic, parsley, bay leaf, or thyme as well as salt and pepper.

The Greeks have such a soup. We have also eaten it in Yugoslavia, in Spain, in Holland, and in France. Some versions of the Italian *minestone* belong in this group. In the United States it is found under names such as county fair soup or United States Senate soup as well as just bean soup. The imaginative cook will vary the type of dried bean, the kind and quantities of other vegetables and will experiment with the seasoning. A few examples, as starters, are given here.

The first step in preparing the following "from scratch" bean soups is the same for all dishes beginning with dried beans. A choice of two soaking methods is given, in which the decision depends on the cook's time schedule. There is no perceptible difference in the end results.

METHOD A: The night before cooking the soup, put 1 pound (approximately 2½ cups) of dried white beans such as navy beans, pea beans, or great northern beans in a large kettle. Add 3 quarts of water and allow the beans to soak overnight.

METHOD B: On the morning of the day you wish to cook the soup put 1 pound of beans (as described in Method A) in a large kettle with 3 quarts of water. Bring slowly to the boiling point; reduce the heat and allow to simmer for a few minutes. Now turn the heat off and allow the beans to stand for 1 to 2 hours.

From this point on the procedure is the same for both soaking methods. Simmer the beans for 1 hour in the water in which they have been soaking, then add the other ingredients as indicated in the following recipes and simmer for an additional 2 hours or longer, until the beans are very tender. Such soups do not suffer from overcooking, and are even better the second day.

SPANISH BEAN SOUP

The distinguishing feature of this soup is the cabbage and red pepper.

1 *pound dried white beans*
1 *large cabbage, chopped*
1 *slice bacon, cut into small pieces*
1 *onion, sliced*

1 *whole red pepper, or*
⅛ *teaspoon (or more) powdered red pepper*
1 *clove garlic, minced (optional)*
Salt to taste

Soak and simmer beans as described in the introduction to this chapter. Add all other ingredients, and continue simmering until beans are very soft, for 2 hours or more.

PER RECIPE: 1880 cal., 115 g. protein, 14 g. fat (3 sat., 6 poly.) FOR 8 SERVINGS, 240 calories per serving

BALKAN BEAN SOUP

1 pound (2½ cups)
   dried white beans
2 stalks celery, chopped
¼ cup tomato purée
2 large onions, chopped

2 large carrots, chopped
2 tablespoons minced
   parsley
¼ cup olive oil
Salt and pepper to taste

Soak and simmer beans as described in the introduction to this chapter, using 3 quarts of water. Add all other ingredients and simmer for 2 hours or longer, until beans are very soft but still whole.

PER RECIPE: 2400 cal., 114 g. protein, 65 g. fat (8 sat., 9 poly.)
FOR 8 SERVINGS, 300 calories per serving

CARRIE'S BEAN SOUP

The first member of our family to add bean soup to her repertoire was our eldest daughter. Not long after her marriage she served it with great pride. This was her own discovery, not just her version of something from her mother's kitchen. Here is her recipe:

2½ cups navy beans
1 ham bone
2 onions, chopped
4 carrots, sliced
2 stalks celery, chopped
1 green pepper, chopped
1 cup tomato purée

⅛ teaspoon mustard
2 (or more) whole
   cloves
4 (or more)
   peppercorns
Salt to taste

Soak and simmer beans as directed in the introduction to this chapter. Add all other ingredients and simmer until beans are tender, for 2 hours or more.

PER RECIPE: 900 cal., 60 g. protein, 9 g. fat (2 sat., 2 poly.)
FOR 8 SERVINGS, 110 calories per serving

MINESTRONE I

This fine soup, as anyone who has traveled in Italy can testify, has as many versions as there are restaurants and *trattorias*, in all degrees from thick soups composed mostly of beans and potatoes to very delicate compositions of fresh vegetables. This one might be found in any part of Italy.

2½ cups navy beans
2 onions, chopped
2 cups sliced celery
4 tablespoons oil
2 cloves garlic, minced
2 tablespoons parsley

4 fresh tomatoes, cut into eighths, or
2 cups canned tomatoes
1 teaspoon salt, or to taste
2 cups shredded cabbage
½ cup grated Parmesan cheese

Soak and simmer beans as described in the introduction to this chapter. Cook onion and celery in oil until golden and add to the beans with all other ingredients except the cabbage and cheese. Simmer until beans are tender, for 2 hours or more, then add the cabbage and cook ½ hour longer.

Serve with grated Parmesan cheese to sprinkle on top.

PER RECIPE: 2300 cal., 114 g. protein, 80 g. fat (13 sat., 32 poly.) FOR 8 SERVINGS, 280 calories per serving

MINESTRONE II

1 onion, chopped
2 tablespoons oil
3 stalks celery, sliced
2 large potatoes, diced
2 teaspoons meat-stock base, or
2 bouillon cubes
2 cups cut green beans

1 cup fresh or frozen peas
Salt and pepper to taste
1 tablespoon chopped parsley
½ cup grated Parmesan cheese

Cook onion in oil until slightly browned, add celery and potatoes. Cover and cook for 10 minutes over low heat. Add 3 quarts of boiling water and meat-stock base or bouillon cubes. Cook 15 minutes longer. Add beans and peas and season with salt, pepper, and parsley. Cook slowly, uncovered, for 15 to 20 minutes more. Serve with grated cheese to sprinkle on top.

PER RECIPE: 1100 cal., 47 g. protein, 45 g. fat (10 sat., 16 poly.) FOR 8 SERVINGS, 140 calories per serving

UNITED STATES SENATE SOUP

2½ cups navy or other beans
1 cooked ham hock, or ½ cup diced cooked ham

½ teaspoon ground cardamom seeds
½ teaspoon celery salt
2 drops Tabasco sauce
2 teaspoons salt or to taste

Soak and simmer beans as directed in the introduction to this chapter. Add all other ingredients and simmer for an additional 2 hours or longer, until the beans are very tender.

PER RECIPE: 1840 cal., 126 g. protein, 17 g. fat (5 sat., 5 poly.) FOR 8 SERVINGS, 230 calories per serving

PASTA E FAGIOLI

(Macaroni and Beans)

This Italian soup is very popular in Italy although almost unknown abroad, partly because it is served more frequently in homes than in restaurants. It appears regularly on the menu for working people—warming, nourishing, and inexpensive. But it also has snob appeal. Experts in the art of dining in Rome can take you to a few fashionable restaurants where *pasta e fagioli* is a specialty. Basically it is soaked and simmered white beans and some form of macaroni in small pieces; the secret is in the seasoning. Here are two versions:

PASTA E FAGIOLI I

1 *pound dried white*
  beans
Salt and pepper to taste
4 *tablespoons olive oil*
¼ *teaspoon rosemary*
  (*optional*)
3 *cloves garlic, minced*

2 *tablespoons chopped*
  parsley or parsley
  flakes
½ *pound elbow*
  macaroni or macaroni
  shells

Soak and simmer beans as described in the introduction to this chapter. Season with salt and pepper. In a small pan heat the oil and rosemary together, remove and discard the rosemary, then add the garlic and parsley and cook for 1 minute over low heat. Add this to the soup and simmer until the beans are tender. Now bring the soup to boiling, add macaroni, and cook until macaroni is done—about 15 minutes.

PER RECIPE: 2940 cal., 130 g. protein, 66 g. fat (8 sat., 8 poly.)
FOR 8 SERVINGS, 370 calories per serving

PASTA E FAGIOLI II

1 *pound dried white*
  beans
½ *cup chopped celery*
1 *clove garlic, minced*
1 *carrot, chopped*
1 *no. 2 can tomatoes*

Salt and pepper to taste
½ *pound macaroni in*
  small pieces
2 *tablespoons olive or*
  other oil

Soak and simmer beans as directed in the introduction to this chapter. Add all other ingredients except macaroni and oil and simmer until the beans are very tender—2 hours or longer.

Cook macaroni separately as directed on the package. Drain and add to bean mixture with oil. Serve very hot.

PER RECIPE: 2840 cal., 137 g. protein, 40 g. fat (4 sat., 20 poly.)
FOR 8 SERVINGS, 360 calories per serving

BEAN SOUP WITH LEEKS

1 *pound navy or other*   2 *tablespoons oil*
  dried white beans   *Salt and pepper*
4 *leeks*

Soak and simmer beans as described in the introduction to
this chapter, continuing to simmer until the beans are tender,
about 3 hours in all. Drain and reserve the cooking water. Pass
half of the beans through a sieve or food mill.

While beans are simmering, cut the white part of the leeks
into thin slices and cook them slowly in the oil until golden
brown. Add the water in which the beans were cooked to the
leeks, and simmer for ½ hour. Then add beans and bean purée
to the soup, season with salt and pepper, and reheat before serving.

PER RECIPE: 1980 cal., 107 g. protein, 36 g. fat (4 sat., 19 poly.)
FOR 8 SERVINGS, 250 calories per serving

SQUASH AND BEAN SOUP

1 *pound dried white*   2 *tablespoons oil*
  beans   1 *pint skim or low fat*
2 *pounds Hubbard,*   *milk*
  buttercup, or other   *Salt and pepper*
  hard yellow squash,
  peeled and cubed

Soak and simmer beans as described in the introduction to
this chapter. Cook squash in oil in covered pan over low heat.
Drain beans, reserving liquid. Put both beans and squash through
food mill or potato ricer, and return purée to bean liquor. Add
milk, season with salt and pepper and serve very hot.

PER RECIPE: 2260 cal., 127 g. protein, 38 g. fat (4 sat., 19 poly.)
FOR 8 SERVINGS, 280 calories per serving

BEAN SOUP WITH CELERY AND ONIONS

1 *pound pea beans*
5–6 *stalks celery, thinly*
  sliced
1 *large onion, sliced*

¼ *cup olive oil*
1 *clove garlic, minced*
½ *teaspoon oregano*
Salt and pepper to taste

Soak and simmer beans as directed in the introduction to this chapter, continuing to simmer beans until tender, about 3 hours in all. When the beans are nearly done, cook the celery and onion in the oil in a separate pan until transparent. Add to the soup with the garlic, oregano, and salt and pepper. Simmer half an hour longer.

PER RECIPE: 2200 cal., 118 g. protein, 63 g. fat (7 sat., 8 poly.) FOR 8 SERVINGS, 280 calories per serving

BEAN AND POTATO PURÉE

1 *pound navy or other*
  dried white beans
1 *pound potatoes*
1 *teaspoon meat-stock*
  base, or
1 *bouillon cube*

2 *cloves garlic, minced*
2 *medium-sized onions,*
  chopped
Salt and pepper to taste
2 *tablespoons flour*
  (*optional*)

Soak and simmer beans as directed in the introduction to this chapter. Peel and cube potatoes and add to beans with meat-stock base or bouillon cube, garlic, and onion. Simmer for 2 hours or longer until beans are very tender. Add water if necessary; this should not be a very thick soup. When beans are done, pass soup through sieve or food mill. Season with salt and pepper and reheat. The soup can be thickened with the flour mixed with water, if desired.

PER RECIPE: 2190 cal., 117 g. protein, 9 g. fat (2 sat., 5 poly.) FOR 8 SERVINGS, 270 calories per serving

LIMA BEAN SOUP

1 cup dried lima beans	1 tablespoon
2 carrots, sliced	Worcestershire sauce
2 onions, sliced	2 teaspoons salt, or to
2 tablespoons minced	taste
parsley	2 tablespoons flour
1 teaspoon peppercorns	2 cups skim milk
or to taste	2–3 drops Tabasco
	sauce (optional)

Soak and simmer beans as described in the introduction to this chapter. Add all other ingredients except the flour and milk and simmer for 2 hours or more until the beans are very soft. Make a paste of the flour and a little of the cold milk. Heat the rest of the milk to scalding. Stir in flour paste and cook and stir until thick. Rub the bean soup through a strainer or put it through a food mill and combine it with the milk mixture just before serving, adjusting seasoning to taste.

PER RECIPE: 920 cal., 58 g. protein, 4 g. fat (1 sat., 2 poly.) FOR 8 SERVINGS, 110 calories per serving

BEAN AND GARLIC SOUP

We ate this soup often in Spain, especially when we were living in the Residence, in Madrid, of the Superior Council on Scientific Research of the Spanish Government. We always knew when it was on the menu as we walked in the door. If you like garlic, it is habit-forming.

1 pound great northern	2 teaspoons salt or to
or other dried	taste
white beans	¼ cup olive oil
8 cloves of garlic	(optional)

Soak and simmer beans as described in the introduction to this chapter, add whole garlic cloves, and continue to simmer until the beans are very tender but still remain whole. In Spain a little olive oil is added to each bowl just before serving. *Beware the cloves of garlic when eating the soup, though most Spaniards would disregard this advice.*

PER RECIPE WITHOUT OIL: 1600 cal., 102 g. protein, 8 g. fat (1 sat., 3 poly.)
PER RECIPE WITH OIL: 1730 cal., 102 g. protein, 22 g. fat (3 sat., 11 poly.)
FOR 8 SERVINGS WITHOUT OIL, 200 calories per serving
FOR 8 SERVINGS WITH OIL, 220 calories per serving

LENTIL SOUP

This soup was served to us in Naples on New Year's Day, following an ancient custom. We were told that this lentil soup would bring us wealth in the New Year, each tiny lentil traditionally representing a coin. The hopeful legend is that the more lentils eaten, the greater the diner's prosperity will be in the New Year.

A similar soup comes from Saudi Arabia, without the tomatoes, but with Swiss chard or spinach added ten minutes before serving. A slice of lemon tops their version.

1 pound lentils	*1 cup tomatoes, stewed*
1 onion, chopped	*or canned*
¼ cup olive oil	*Salt and pepper to taste*

Treat lentils to the same soak-and-simmer procedure described for beans in the introduction to this chapter. Cook lentils 2 hours or longer. While the lentils are simmering, fry onion in a separate pan until soft. Add tomatoes and simmer for 5 minutes. When lentils are done, combine with onion-tomato mixture and reheat, seasoning with salt and pepper.

PER RECIPE: 2140 cal., 116 g. protein, 61 g. fat (7 sat., 7 poly.)
FOR 8 SERVINGS, 270 calories per serving

LENTIL SOUP WITH PRUNES

A friend of ours recalled that in her girlhood in Luxembourg, lentils were cooked with prunes. It sounded like a curious combination, but, encouraged by a similar recipe in *The Wonderful World of Cooking* by Edward Harris Heth, we experimented and liked the results.

1 pound (2½ cups) lentils	*15 pitted prunes*
3 slices (¼ pound) Canadian bacon, or	*2 tablespoons brown sugar*
¼ pound cooked ham	*2 tablespoons vinegar*
2 onions, chopped	*1 pinch thyme*
1 large carrot, chopped	*Salt to taste*
	1 lemon, sliced

Soak and simmer lentils in the manner described for beans in the introduction to this chapter. Add all other ingredients except lemon and simmer for 2 hours or longer until the soup is thick and the lentils tender. Serve with a slice of lemon in each soup bowl.

PER RECIPE: 2480 cal., 132 g. protein, 68 g. fat (23 sat., 8 poly.) FOR 8 SERVINGS, 310 calories per serving

SPLIT PEA SOUP

First the baked ham is enjoyed; then the scraps are used in scalloped potatoes or ham salad sandwiches; finally the remnants are used for split pea soup and only then can the family dog have the bone to gnaw on.

1 pound (2¼ cups) split peas	*Salt to taste*
Ham bone or turkey carcass	*¼ cup flour*

Soak peas as described for beans in the introduction to this chapter. Add ham bone or turkey carcass and simmer for 2 hours or longer. Pour the soup through a colander to remove the bones. Chill it and remove the congealed fat from the top.

Reheat the soup. Taste for seasoning and add salt if needed. Mix flour with ½ cup cold water to make a smooth paste. Stir the flour paste into the soup, and continue stirring over heat until soup is smooth and boiling.

PER RECIPE: 1780 cal., 146 g. protein, 5 g. fat (1 sat., 3 poly.) FOR 8 SERVINGS, 220 calories per serving

BLACK BEAN SOUP

1 pound black beans
½ cup chopped onion
1 cup chopped celery
    and leaves
½ cup chopped carrot
1 green pepper, chopped
2 tomatoes, cubed

1 ham bone or turkey
    carcass
2 bay leaves
Salt and paprika to
    taste
3 tablespoons oil
2 tablespoons flour
1 lemon, sliced

Soak and simmer beans as described in the introduction to this chapter. Add all ingredients except oil, flour, and lemon. Simmer 2 hours or longer until the beans are very tender. Put through a colander and chill. Remove congealed fat from the top. Blend oil and flour and stir it into the soup. Taste for seasoning, and serve with thin slices of lemon.

An alternate method is to cook the ham bone or turkey carcass a day ahead in 3 quarts of water for an hour. Chill overnight and remove congealed fat. Soak beans overnight. Drain the beans in the morning and put them to simmer in the ham or turkey stock with the other vegetables and the bay leaves. This method eliminates the necessity for chilling the entire soup to get rid of the fat, since it has been removed from the stock. When the beans are tender, the blended oil and flour can be stirred in and the soup served immediately.

PER RECIPE: 2730 cal., 153 g. protein, 51 g. fat (5 sat., 26 poly.) FOR 8 SERVINGS, 260 calories per serving

ERWTENSOEP

This well-known soup is a Dutch tradition, usually made with smoked sausage, but given here with ready-to-eat frankfurters to simplify preparation.

3 cups split green peas	1 cup chopped celery
2 pig's feet	and leaves
3 leeks, sliced	1 celery root or
2 onions, sliced	celeriac, diced
2 tablespoons oil	1 pound frankfurters,
2 tablespoons chopped	ready to eat
parsley	Salt and pepper to taste

Soak and simmer the peas as described for beans in the introduction to this chapter. Add the pig's feet and simmer for 2 hours. Brown the leeks and onion in oil and add to the soup with the parsley, celery, and celery root. Cut the frankfurters into pieces, add to the soup, and season with salt and pepper. Can be made a day ahead, if desired, and reheated. It is traditionally served with pumpernickel bread.

PER RECIPE: 4900 cal., 272 g. protein, 199 g. fat (62 sat., 31 poly.)
FOR 10 SERVINGS, 490 calories per serving

SOUP OF FRESH GREEN PEAS

2 pounds fresh peas in	2 cups chicken stock
the shell, or	2 tablespoons flour
2 packages frozen peas	Salt and paprika to taste
1 onion, chopped	2 cups skim milk

Shell the peas and cook them with the onion in the stock until soft enough to mash easily—from 10 to 20 minutes, depending on the maturity of the peas. Put through a potato ricer or food mill. Make a paste of the flour with a little water and add it to the soup. Stir over medium heat until the soup is boiling. Season with salt and paprika. Add the milk and serve when hot.

PER RECIPE: 590 cal., 46 g. protein, 2 g. fat (trace sat., 1 poly.) FOR 4 SERVINGS, 150 calories per serving

BEAN CURD SOUP I

Bean curd is one of the products of the centuries-old methods used by the Chinese to make soybeans more edible both in flavor and digestibility. It is sold in cakes and can be found in our big cities where there are Chinese or Japanese food shops. It is also available in cans, though the fresh product is certainly better.

It can be cooked as a vegetable, as a meat, or with seafood, and it can also be used to replace noodles in soup. Here is the simplest version.

1 cake (4"×1") bean curd
3 cups consommé

Slice or dice the bean curd, heat it in consommé, and serve.

PER RECIPE: 220 cal., 25 g. protein, 11 g. fat (2 sat., 7 poly.) FOR 3 SERVINGS, 70 calories per serving

BEAN CURD SOUP II

1 cake (4"×1") bean curd, in 1-inch cubes
⅛ pound lean pork, cut in thin across-the-grain slices
½ pound Chinese celery-cabbage (bok choy), sliced

2 slices ginger
1 (6½-oz.) can diced bamboo shoots
½ teaspoon monosodium glutamate
Salt and pepper to taste

Add all ingredients to 1 quart of boiling water and simmer for 10 minutes.

PER RECIPE: 430 cal., 42 g. protein, 21 g. fat (6 sat., 8 poly.) FOR 4 SERVINGS, 110 calories per serving

BEAN SPROUT SOUP

Another bean product which comes to us from the Orient is bean sprouts, now commonly available in cans. They can also be grown in the home, without too much know-how, from either soybeans or mung beans (see page 46).

2 green onions and tops	Salt to taste, speck of
1 clove garlic, minced	pepper
¼ pound lean beef, cut	½ teaspoon ground,
into small, thin slices	roasted sesame seeds
4 tablespoons soy sauce	3 cups fresh or canned
	bean sprouts

Chop onions (reserving tops). Add onion and garlic to the meat with half of the soy sauce, the salt, pepper, and sesame seeds. Mix together and cook until the meat is well seared, about 5 minutes.

If fresh bean sprouts are used, prepare them by removing the hairlike end on each sprout. Wash well and add to the meat. If canned bean sprouts are used, drain and rinse in cold water, then add to the meat. Mix and cook for 3 minutes. Add 2 quarts of water and the rest of the soy sauce to the beef and sprouts and cook for 30 minutes or until the sprouts and meat are tender. Five minutes before serving, cut the green tops of the onions into 1-inch lengths and add to the soup.

PER RECIPE: 260 cal., 34 g. protein, 6 g. fat (2 sat., trace poly.) FOR 8 SERVINGS, 30 calories per serving

COUNTY FAIR SOUP

There are many good canned bean soups on the market. They are delicious when served according to the directions on the can, but also lend themselves to home variations such as this one.

2 slices bacon
3 tablespoons chopped
onion
1 tablespoon oil
⅛ teaspoon thyme

1 (10¾-oz.) can
condensed vegetable
bean soup
½ cup cooked cut green
beans

Cook bacon until crisp. Remove from pan and crumble; discard drippings. In the same pan cook the onion in oil until tender. Season with thyme and add soup, 1 soup can of water, and the green beans. Stir often while heating. Top each serving with crumbled bacon.

PER RECIPE: 620 cal., 27 g. protein, 22 g. fat (11 sat., 1 poly.)
FOR 3 SERVINGS, 210 calories per serving

CURRY SOUP

2 medium-sized onions,
finely chopped
2 tablespoons oil
3 tablespoons flour
1 tablespoon curry
powder, or to taste

6 cups of bean soup, or
2 (10½-oz.) cans
vegetable bean soup
3 tablespoons chopped
parsley

Cook the onions slowly in the oil until golden. Blend in the flour and curry powder, mix well, then add the soup, stirring continuously until boiling. Reduce the heat and simmer for 10 minutes. Rub through a strainer, reheat, and serve with parsley sprinkled on top.

PER RECIPE: 1650 cal., 59 g. protein, 80 g. fat (7 sat., 26 poly.)
FOR 6 SERVINGS, 280 calories per serving

GREEN AND BROWN SOUP

1 (10¾-oz.) can vegetable bean soup
1 (10-oz.) package frozen Italian beans

Prepare soup as directed on the can. When boiling, add frozen beans, bring again to the boil. Cover and simmer, following package directions, until green beans are just tender. Taste for seasoning—a little more salt may be required.

PER RECIPE: 370 cal., 21 g. protein, 6 g. fat (1 sat., 4 poly.)
FOR 4 SERVINGS, 90 calories per serving

QUICK SUNDAY SUPPER SOUP

2 (10¾-oz.) cans cream of celery soup
2 cups cooked drained navy or other beans

Prepare soup as directed on the can, add the beans and heat thoroughly.

PER RECIPE: 1030 cal., 45 g. protein, 35 g. fat (19 sat., 1 poly.)
FOR 8 SERVINGS, 130 calories per serving

LOMBARDY BEAN SOUP

4 slices of bread, toasted
1 can of bean soup, prepared according to directions on the can, or
1 can of cooked beans, seasoned with ½ teaspoon onion flakes
Freshly ground black pepper to taste

Put the freshly prepared toast in soup plates, pour the hot soup or the seasoned cooked beans (heated) over the toast, and season with pepper.

PER RECIPE: 490 cal., 22 g. protein, 7 g. fat (2 sat., 4 poly.)
FOR 4 SERVINGS, 120 calories per serving

BEAN POTS

Our slogan is "a good bean pot in every kitchen"—and we hope that the pot will have much use—for ordinary baked beans and other baked dishes of beans and their relatives that come out of the pot are nutritious, delicious, cheap, and easy. Bostonians traditionally eat the same kind of baked beans as a main dish every Saturday night; with the variety offered below the frequency of enjoying beans baked in a pot could easily be twice that.

Besides beans, you need a pot to start with. Choose one of the same family of design as the early pottery of the province of Kansu, in northern China, or found in the Palace of Minos in Crete, both from about three thousand years before Christ. A bean pot of this type can be had for a small sum at your neighborhood hardware store. Or grace your kitchen with one of modern design—it may also serve for flowers or as a casserole for some other baked dishes. The bean pot may be of old-fashioned brown stoneware, glazed earthenware, or of colored Pyrex or steel clad with the new kind of tough baked-on enamel. The material does not matter so long as the pot resists heat, is well glazed inside, has a lid, and is quite deep.

To look at, a dried bean isn't exciting, and a tentative bite in the raw state offers no hint of the cooked taste. Even when the beans are softened overnight the bite test is not rewarding. But magic is worked in the bean pot: left unattended in a slow oven for a few hours, those pallid objects in a watery solution change to plump brown morsels of flavor in a rich sauce. Except in ultra-sophisticated circles it is more fashionable to rave about complicated and expensive foods than to wax enthusiastic about baked beans, but it is astonishing to see what quantities will disappear if you venture to serve them for company.

There is no better combination with baked beans than the classical one of New England—codfish cakes and brown bread. But you don't have to put those foils alongside the baked beans to have them enjoyed by all. "Bean feed" often means baked beans and cole slaw, and this teen-age favorite appeals to all ages. Excellent combinations with baked beans are broccoli (cold or hot, with or without Hollandaise sauce), spinach, braised celery, zucchini, cauliflower, sliced tomatoes, a big bowl of green salad. "Double beans" are good: baked beans served with snap or wax beans. Baked beans and fried bananas make a surprisingly good combination, especially if there are lots of lettuce and celery on the side. Come to think of it, baked beans combine well with almost anything except heavy starchy foods such as potatoes, spaghetti, corn, and Hubbard or acorn squash. In many parts of the world beans and rice are a favorite dish.

In the United States there are many recipes for baked beans, but the best known and widely appreciated is that from the "home of the bean and the cod." There are many variants but the following recipe is typical:

BOSTON BAKED BEANS

3 cups dried pea beans	3 tablespoons sugar
¼ pound lean salt pork	½ teaspoon dry mustard
1 small onion	⅓ cup molasses
1 tablespoon salt	

The quantities given fill a 2-quart bean pot. Any 2-quart ovenproof dish with a cover can be used, but should be checked fairly frequently to make sure that the beans do not become too dry.

Soak and simmer beans as described in the introduction to

the chapter on soups. Meanwhile, pour boiling water over salt pork and allow to stand for 10 minutes. Drain and cut pork into small pieces. Discard rind or place it on top of the beans. Slice the onion and put it in the bottom of the bean pot. Add the pork bits. Drain the beans, reserving the liquid, and add to the pot. Dissolve salt, sugar, mustard, and molasses in 1 cup of hot bean liquor and pour into pot, adding more bean liquor or boiling water until the beans are just covered. Cover the pot, and bake the beans in a slow (250°) oven for 6 to 8 hours, adding boiling water as necessary.

PER RECIPE: 2700 cal., 142 g. protein, 38 g. fat (12 sat., 9 poly.) FOR 8 SERVINGS, 340 calories per serving

FRIJOLES DE OLLA

(Beans in a Pot)

Beans are so great a favorite in Mexico that the terms *nacionales* and *frijoles* are often used interchangeably. The basic Mexican recipe for baked beans is given here. The baked beans are eaten as such but it is customary to prepare enough so that there will be an abundant leftover for use in other ways: *refritos*, for example (recipe in chapter on VEGETABLES). In a simple home in Mexico a pot of these beans is always on hand.

1 pound (2½ cups) pinto, pink, or other beans
¼ pound salt pork, cut into bits
Salt to taste

Soak and simmer beans as directed in the introduction to the chapter on soups. Transfer them with their liquor to a bean pot, add salt pork, and simmer over low heat for 4 to 6 hours, adding boiling water as necessary. Or cover the pot and bake in a slow (250°) oven. When nearly done, taste for seasoning and add salt if desired.

PER RECIPE: 2390 cal., 106 g. protein, 104 g. fat (34 sat., 10 poly.)
FOR 10 SERVINGS, 240 calories per serving

BEANS SÃO PAULO

Brazilians eat more beans than almost any other people, and the variety of their recipes is legion. Here is a favorite recipe for baked white beans that reputedly hails from the city of São Paulo.

1 pound navy beans	Salt and pepper to taste
1 onion, sliced	2 tablespoons chopped
1 clove garlic, minced	parsley
½ pound Canadian	12 pitted green olives
bacon, or lean ham,	
cubed	

Soak and simmer beans according to directions in the introduction to the chapter on SOUPS. Drain them, reserving the liquor. Place sliced onion and garlic in the bottom of the bean pot, add beans, bacon or ham, and 1 teaspoon salt. Pour bean liquor over the beans until they are covered. Bake in a slow (250°) oven for 3 hours or more. Taste for saltiness, adding more salt if necessary with pepper and parsley. Serve with sliced green olives on top.

PER RECIPE: 2170 cal., 97 g. protein, 49 g. fat (15 sat., 7 poly.) FOR 8 SERVINGS, 270 calories per serving

KEEWATIN BEANS

Named for the well-seasoned, homemade Italian-type of sausage which comes from Keewatin, Minnesota.

3 cups navy beans
1 pound pork sausage or ½ pound summer or cervelat
sausage
Salt to taste (depending on seasoning of sausage)

Soak and simmer beans as directed in the introduction to the chapter on SOUPS. Cut sausage into bite-sized bits and brown in skillet, discarding the fat which cooks out. Combine sausage and beans in bean pot with enough of the bean liquor to almost cover, and bake at 250° for 2 hours or longer. After an hour of cooking, taste for saltiness and add salt if needed.

PER RECIPE: 3750 cal., 196 g. protein, 151 g. fat (56 sat., 18 poly.)
FOR 8 SERVINGS, 470 calories per serving

BAKED LIMA BEANS

2 cups dry lima beans
2 onions, sliced
5 carrots, chopped
¼ pound ham, cut into
    small pieces

Salt and pepper to taste
2 tablespoons chopped
    parsley

Soak and simmer beans as directed in the introduction to the chapter on SOUPS. Drain beans, reserving liquor, and transfer them to a 2-quart bean pot. Add onion, carrot, and ham; mix well. Add bean liquor to cover beans, season with salt and pepper, and bake at 350° for 1½ hours. Stir in chopped parsley just before serving.

PER RECIPE: 1630 cal., 103 g. protein, 16 g. fat (4 sat., 4 poly.)
FOR 8 SERVINGS, 200 calories per serving

BEANS BRETONNE

Here is a recipe for French (Brittany) baked beans.

2 cups navy beans
1 chicken bouillon cube
1 (6-oz.) can tomato
    paste
1 onion, finely chopped

1 clove garlic, minced
1 (4-oz.) jar pimento,
    drained and chopped
2 tablespoons oil
Salt and paprika to taste

Soak and simmer beans as directed in the introduction to the chapter on SOUPS. Drain the beans and put them in a bean pot, reserving the liquor. Dissolve the bouillon cube in 1 cup of the bean liquor, combine with the tomato paste, and pour over the beans. Add the other ingredients and enough bean liquor to cover the beans, cover the pot, and bake in a slow (250°) oven for 2 hours or longer.

PER RECIPE: 1700 cal., 87 g. protein, 36 g. fat (3 sat., 18 poly.) FOR 8 SERVINGS, 210 calories per serving

OHIO BAKED BEANS

1 *pound navy beans*	½ *cup brown sugar*
¼ *pound bacon, cut into*	1 *cup catsup*
bits	1 *(6-oz.) can tomato*
1 *bottle pickled onions*	*sauce*

Soak and simmer beans according to directions in the introduction to the chapter on SOUPS. Drain beans, reserving liquor. Place beans in 2-quart bean pot in layers with bacon and pickled onions. Combine remaining ingredients and pour over the beans, adding bean liquor if necessary to bring level of liquid to top of beans. Cover bean pot and bake at 250° for 5 to 6 hours. Uncover for last hour of baking, adding more bean liquor as needed.

PER RECIPE: 3040 cal., 116 g. protein, 87 g. fat (27 sat., 11 poly.) FOR 8 SERVINGS, 380 calories per serving

AMY'S BAKED BEANS

1 *pound navy beans*	1 *tablespoon salt*
1 *onion, sliced*	1 *teaspoon dry mustard*
½ *pound beef stewing*	½ *cup catsup*
meat, cut into ½-inch	1 *tablespoon*
cubes	*Worcestershire sauce*
½ *cup molasses*	

Soak and simmer beans as directed in the introduction to the chapter on SOUPS. Drain the beans, reserving liquor. Place onion in the bottom of a 2-quart bean pot. Mix beans and beef together and add to the pot. Combine all other ingredients and add to the pot with enough bean liquor to cover the beans. Bake at 250° for 6 to 8 hours, adding more liquid as needed.

PER RECIPE: 2490 cal., 153 g. protein, 26 g. fat (10 sat., 4 poly.) FOR 8 SERVINGS, 310 calories per serving

QUICK LIMA BEAN POT

½ pound frankfurters, cut into 1-inch pieces
1 cup diced celery
½ cup chopped onion
2 tablespoons oil
2 (10-oz.) packages frozen lima beans

2 teaspoons prepared mustard
1 (10½-oz.) can tomato soup
1 tablespoon brown sugar
1 tablespoon vinegar
Salt to taste

Cook frankfurters, celery, and onion in oil in a skillet for 5 minutes, stirring frequently. Transfer to bean pot and add remaining ingredients with ½ cup water. Cover and bake for 45 minutes in medium (350°) oven. Stir once or twice; add more water if necessary. Season with salt.

PER RECIPE: 1810 cal., 64 g. protein, 98 g. fat (24 sat., 21 poly.) FOR 6 SERVINGS, 300 calories per serving

HUNGARIAN BEAN STEW

2 cups great northern beans
1 cup pearl barley
2 carrots, sliced
2 parsnips, diced
1 medium-sized onion
1 green pepper, chopped

1 tomato, chopped
2 tablespoons oil
1 teaspoon paprika
2 tablespoons flour
½ pound smoked sausage, sliced
Salt to taste

Soak and simmer beans as directed in the introduction to the chapter on soups. Add barley, carrots, parsnips, the whole onion, green pepper, and tomato; cover and simmer for 1 hour. Heat oil in frying pan, add paprika and flour, stir until browned, then dilute with ½ cup water, and add it to the stew. Put the sausage slices in the bottom of a bean pot, pour the stew over it. Cover and cook in moderate (350°) oven for an additional hour. Taste for seasoning before serving, adding salt if necessary.

PER RECIPE: 2100 cal., 86 g. protein, 36 g. fat (3 sat., 18 poly.) FOR 8 SERVINGS, 260 calories per serving

POTTAGE OF LENTILS

According to Leah W. Leonard in *Jewish Cookery*, it was for a dish of this sort that Esau sold his birthright. Variations of this lamb and lentil stew are found today in many eastern Mediterranean countries.

1 *pound lentils*
6 *medium-sized onions,*
   sliced
1 *pound lamb shoulder,*
   cut into ½-inch cubes
¼ *cup oil*
4 *carrots, chopped*

1 *green pepper, seeded*
   and chopped
1 *(1-pound) can*
   tomatoes
2 *stalks celery, sliced*
Salt and pepper to taste

Soak and simmer lentils as described for beans in the introduction to the chapter on SOUPS. Fry onion and meat in oil for about 10 minutes. Drain lentils, reserving liquor. Combine lentils with meat mixture and vegetables in 2-quart bean pot, adding liquor to bring the level just above lentil mixture. Season with salt and pepper. Cover and bake in slow (250°) oven for 2 hours.

PER RECIPE: 3250 cal., 222 g. protein, 66 g. fat (18 sat., 32 poly.) FOR 8 SERVINGS, 410 calories per serving

CASSOULET
BEAN STEW IN THE
GRAND MANNER

Cassoulet, essentially a humble peasant dish, an old favorite in
the South of France, has lately been acclaimed one of the true
native glories of French cookery. Even snob accounts of *la cuisine française* wax poetic about cassoulet and give lengthy recipes
for its preparation. Alexander Watt in *Paris Bistro Cookery*
(1957, MacGibbon & Kee, London) lists restaurants in Paris
recommended for cassoulet.

Cassoulet is an elaborate bean stew, which sounds pretty ple-
beian, and it is not too easy to decide when a bean stew with
a lot of meat in it should be labeled cassoulet. Perhaps it is
useful to specify some ingredients that are never in a real cassoulet. It never contains potatoes, rice, pasta, or other farina-
ceous items. If meat, fowl, or sausage is added to the Italian
pasta e fagioli (macaroni-type pasta and beans), or to the bean
and rice stews popular in Spain and Latin America, the result
is not cassoulet, though it can be good. Further, real cassoulet
never contains beef, veal, seafood, or any members of the cabbage and cauliflower family, though these too can be used to
make good bean stews. Butter and cheese do not belong in
cassoulet.

These exclusions still leave plenty of scope. Beans are essential, of course, and most authorities specify that only white beans can be used; there are recipes that specify kidney beans, but it is doubtful that this means red or Mexican kidney beans. Beans are only the beginning. Cassoulet always contains garlic and generous amounts of onions and strong-flavored meat, fowl, or sausage, frequently all three. Pork, mutton, and lamb are the proper meats; goose, sometimes "preserved,"* is the proper fowl; and the sausage is of the hearty, solid type, meaning that frankfurters, Vienna sausage, or what is called Bologna in the United States will not qualify. Tomatoes or tomato paste are sometimes added. Herbs and spices are commonly used—a bay leaf or two, some thyme, a couple of cloves, pepper, perhaps parsley. Rosemary, oregano, nutmeg, turmeric, cinnamon, and mustard *never* go into cassoulet.

Authentic French recipes for cassoulet never mention chicken or turkey, probably because chicken is a little bland for the powerful effect admired in cassoulet and turkey is a too recent introduction into France to have been considered. But turkey, plain or smoked, is good in cassoulet and wild game is even better. Cassoulet is a robust dish that welcomes well-flavored ingredients, especially when it contains plenty of beans. Pheasant and mushrooms are lost in cassoulet.

For accompaniment, good French-type bread and a dry white wine are held to be essentials. We agree about the bread: the crustier the better. As to the wine, at least one authority advises a dry red and we find this agreeable, but perhaps a cold white wine is a better foil for such heavy food. And, also as a foil, cassoulet should be accompanied by a big bowl of green salad with plain oil and vinegar dressing; sugar, mustard, mayonnaise,

---

* "Preserved" goose here means *confit d'oie*, as prepared in the South of France. Properly, the goose is killed on St. Martin's Day, November 11. It is cleaned and cut up into joints, the fat is cut off and saved; the rest is salted on all sides and put into an earthenware pot with a weight on top where it stays in a cool, dry place for ten days. Then, in a big, heavy saucepan, the fat set aside earlier is used to make a bed on which the pieces of goose are placed. The whole is cooked over a slow fire for about one and a half hours. The pieces of goose are then removed to an earthenware jar and the strained fat is poured over them. The *confit* will keep for months in a cool dry place.

catsup, cheese, or other additions to the salad dressing spoil the lightness and refreshment. If a more highly flavored salad dressing is desired, rub the bowl with garlic, add a few drops of onion juice, and a pinch of pepper as well as the usual salt. Fresh fruit or a not-too-sweet fruit compote will finish off the meal, and perhaps a cup of strong coffee will help everyone to stay awake.

Here are some of the best accounts and recipes for *le cassoulet* in our library. See also the recipe, with cooking details, in *Life* Magazine for October 8, 1965. But let us start off with

LANGUEDOC CASSOULET—WAVERLEY ROOT

The outstanding dish of Languedoc is cassoulet, white beans cooked in a pot with various types of meat, which takes its name from the dish in which it is cooked, the *cassole*—an old-fashioned word no longer in current use. Originally it belonged to the family of farm-kitchen dishes, like *pot-au-feu*, which remain on the back of the stove indefinitely, serving as a sort of catchall for anything edible that the cook may toss into the pot. Anatole France claimed in his *Histoire Comique* that the cassoulet he used to eat in a favorite establishment in Paris had been cooking for twenty years. It is to be doubted that any restaurant could be found today in which the stoves had not been allowed to cool off in that length of time. Modern fuels may be more convenient to handle than the farmer's wood, but they are too expensive not to be turned off between meals.

This sort of a dish is obviously likely to vary with the individual cook, or even with what the individual cook happens to have at hand (my own cook makes a first-rate cassoulet, but the ingredients are likely to be different every time). The one thing that does not change is the beans. Nevertheless, you can work up a hot argument among cassoulet-fanciers at any time about the ingredients of the real cassoulet. It is a subject as touchy as the correct composition of a mint julep in certain regions of the American South. With the caution that this is a most variable dish, even when made on the same spot by the same person, what seems to be majority opinion on the standard varieties of the dish, which then serve as points of departure for individual fantasy, is offered here:

There are three main types of cassoulet, those of Castelnaudary, Carcassonne, and Toulouse, of which the first seems to have been the original dish. It is therefore, in principle at least, the simplest, combining with the beans only fresh pork, ham, a bit of pork shoulder, sausage, and fresh pork cracklings. Carcassonne starts with this, and adds hunks of leg of mutton to the mixture (in season, there may also be partridge in this cassoulet). Toulouse also starts out with the Castelnaudary base, but adds to it not only mutton (in this case from less expensive cuts), but also bacon, Toulouse sausage, and preserved goose. The last ingredient may sometimes be replaced by preserved duck, or there may even be samples of both.

This would seem to make everything plain—Castelnaudary, only pork; Carcassonne, distinguished by mutton; Toulouse, distinguished by goose. However, an authority I have just consulted, which lays down these distinctions very sternly, then goes on to give two recipes for cassoulet de Castelnaudary; one of them contains mutton and the other contains goose. The conclusion that must be drawn is that cassoulet is what you find it.

The only invariable rule that can be stated about cassoulet, with whatever name it may be ticketed on the menu, seems to be that it is a dish of white beans, preferably those of Pamiers or Cazères, cooked in a pot with some form of pork and sausage. After that it is a case of fielder's choice. Other points various forms of cassoulet are likely to have in common are: the use of goose fat in the cooking; seasoning that includes assorted herbs, an onion with cloves stuck into it, and garlic; and enough liquid to give it plenty of thick juice, sometimes provided by meat bouillon. The approved method is first to cook meat and beans together—they are likely to enter the process at different times, depending on their relative cooking speeds—and to finish the process by putting the whole thing into a pot, coating the surface with bread crumbs, which gives it a crunchy golden crust, and finishing the cooking very slowly, preferably in a baker's oven. There is a tradition that the crust should be broken and stirred into the whole steaming mass again seven times during the cooking.

LE CASSOULET DE TOULOUSE

André L. Simon

2 *pounds shoulder of mutton*	1 *or* 2 *cloves garlic*
1 *pound rinds of pork* (couennes grasses)	10 *pieces of* confit d'oie
¼ *pound onions*	1 *quart dried beans*
1 *fresh Toulouse sausage*	¼ *pound fat salt pork*
1 *bay leaf*	1 *sprig thyme*
	Salt and pepper
	1 *pint white wine*

This is a "robust" dish such as French peasants, who do not possess modern squeamish stomachs, love. It should be enjoyed in good company, at leisure, and washed down with copious draughts of good white wine, followed by a cup of black coffee and a glass of Armagnac brandy.

Soak the beans overnight. Have a heavy iron saucepan—such are *de rigueur* for all these slow-cooked dishes—and line the bottom with the rinds of fat fresh salt pork. Cover these with the drained beans and the white wine, adding sufficient water to completely cover the beans. Salt with moderation. Add the herbs and a little pepper. Cover and cook gently 1½ hours when the beans will be half-cooked.

Brown the mutton, cut into pieces, in the fat rendered by the salt pork which has been gently fried to extract it. Add the sliced onions and the minced or grated garlic. Add all this to the beans, with the gravy from the mutton, cover and cook until mutton is done as well as the beans. Now add the pieces of *confit d'oie* and 3 tablespoons of its succulent fat. Turn all into a large earthenware pan and set in a fairly hot oven when, after a short while, a "skin" will form on the surface. Mix this, very carefully, with the beans and replace in the oven. Repeat this skinning and mixing operation six times, adding the browned sausage after the fifth mixing. Do not disturb the seventh "skin." Cut the sausage into rather thick slices, serve on top of the casserole, and sprinkle all with finely chopped parsley. Serve in baking dish, VERY hot.

CASSOULET DU LANGUEDOC

Alfred Guérot

1 quart kidney beans
½ pound lean breast
    pork
½ pound bacon
1 medium-sized carrot
1 medium-sized onion
1 clove
Bouquet garni*
3 cloves garlic, crushed
Salt and pepper

¾ pound pork chops
1 preserved goose
½ pound uncooked
    garlic sausage
4 sliced onions
5 tablespoons
    concentrated tomato
    paste
2 tablespoons white
    bread crumbs

Soak the beans in cold water for 2 hours, drain, and put into a pan with breast of pork and 4 quarts cold water. Heat slowly to boiling point, skim, boil for 5 minutes, and drain.

Rinse out the pan and put the pork and beans back into it with 2½ quarts cold water, ½ teaspoon salt, bacon, carrot, onion studded with clove, and bouquet garni. Simmer gently on very low heat for 1½ hours. In another pan, brown pork chops in preserved goose fat. Season with salt and pepper. When nicely browned on all sides, remove and, in the same pan, lightly fry the sliced onion. As soon as they become transparent, add garlic, toss; add tomato purée and ½ cup liquid from the beans. Simmer very gently for 5 minutes.

Remove carrot, onion, and bouquet garni from the bean pot. Leave enough liquid to cover the beans, add pork chops, sausage,

* Herbs such as thyme, bay leaf, and parsley tied together in a small piece of cheesecloth.

and fried onion. Cover and simmer on a low flame for 1 hour.

Remove all the meats. Slice the pork, cut the preserved goose into small pieces, skin sausage, and cut into round slices.

Line a deep earthenware pot with bacon and put in a layer of beans. On top of this put a layer of various meats with some of their sauce. Put more beans on top and continue to fill the pot with alternate layers, seasoning each one with a little freshly ground pepper. On the last layer of beans, lay slices of pork, bacon, and sliced garlic sausage. Sprinkle with bread crumbs, pour a little goose fat over them, and cook in a moderate (350°) oven for 35 minutes. Serves 8 to 10.

CASSOULET MÉNAGÈRE
Louis Diat

Cassoulet originally was a specialty of the southwestern part of France, from Toulouse, which lies west of the Pyrenees, to Carcassone, where the mountains start to go down to the shores of the Mediterranean. Toulouse, Castelnaudary, Carcassonne, and many other towns have their own preferred combinations of ingredients, and each, of course, considers its own the best. Thus there are various combinations of mutton, pork, goose, duck, sausage, and white beans, and in some places even the meat of an old partridge, when in season, is added. But, regardless of whatever else goes into the casserole, dried white beans and garlic sausages are always included.

Cassoulet is a hearty, inexpensive dish, perfect for a large family of hungry youngsters and grownups. But it takes a long time to cook and should have an oven with a steady even heat to bring it to its final tender succulence.

As people have moved to other parts of France from the Haute-Garonne Department where cassoulet is a specialty, they have taken their recipes with them until now cassoulet is served in homes and restaurants everywhere. The following recipe is typical and generally popular. Instead of lamb, roast loin of pork cut in slices or sliced goose may be used. In some sections goose is a traditional ingredient.

2 pounds breast, neck or shoulder of lamb, cut into pieces

2½–3 cups dried beans soaked in cold water for a few hours

½ pound saucisson or pork sausage with garlic (if obtainable)

3 ounces fat salt pork and rind, diced

½ tablespoon salt

3 tablespoons lard

A little pepper

2 onions, finely chopped

½ cup canned tomatoes (or 3 fresh tomatoes, peeled, seeded, and chopped)

2 cloves garlic, crushed

1 faggot (parsley, celery, bay leaf, thyme)

3 tablespoons bread crumbs

1 tablespoon chopped parsley

Drain beans, put in saucepan, cover with water, add ½ tablespoon salt and the *saucisson*. Bring to a boil and cook slowly about 1 hour, removing *saucisson* after it has cooked for 35 minutes. Parboil pork dice 5 minutes, drain and sauté in a little lard until golden brown. Remove them and set aside. Put lard in saucepan, heat very hot, and add pieces of lamb seasoned with salt and pepper. Brown them on all sides. Drain off fat, add onion, and cook with meat until they are golden brown. Add just enough water to cover meat, bring to a boil, add tomatoes, garlic, faggot, and pork dice and cook slowly for about half an hour, adding salt, if needed. Drain the beans and add. Cover pan and cook slowly 1½ to 2 hours longer or until meat and beans are done. Discard faggot. About 15 minutes before serving, rub the insides of individual casseroles (or one large one) with cut garlic. Cut *saucisson* in slices. Into each casserole put some meat with some beans, some slices of *saucisson*, some salt pork dice and pour sauce over. Sprinkle with bread crumbs and a little butter and put under broiler or in a hot oven until brown. Serve sprinkled with chopped parsley. Serves 5 or 6.

CASSOULET
Escoffier

Set one quart of dried white beans to cook with two quarts of water, ⅓ ounce of salt, one carrot, one onion stuck with a clove, one herb bunch, six garlic cloves, and ⅔ pound of fresh pork rind, blanched and tied together. Boil; skim; cover, and cook gently for 1 hour. At the end of this time, add ⅔ pound breast or belly of pork, and a sausage with garlic, of the same weight as the pork. Salt the beans very moderately, allowing for the reduction which they have ultimately to undergo.

Complete the cooking of the whole gently.

Or fry gently in lard 1 pound of shoulder of mutton, and the same weight of breast of mutton; both cut into pieces 1½ ounces in weight.

This done, drain away half the grease; add 2 chopped onions and 2 crushed cloves of garlic, and fry again until the onions have acquired a slight color. Now pour in ⅙ pint of good tomato purée; moisten the meat, enough to cover, with the cooking liquor of dried white beans, and cook gently in the oven for 1½ hours at least.

Or garnish the bottom and sides of some "cocottes" or deep dishes with bacon rind; fill these with alternate layers of the pieces of mutton, the beans, the bacon cut into dice, and the sausage cut into round slices.

Sprinkle the surface with "raspings," and set the "gratin" to form in a moderate oven for 1 hour; taking care to baste from time to time with some reserved dried white beans cooking liquor.

CASSOULET
Peter Gray

This is a fabulous stew coming from *Les Landes*, which is that region of France in which geese are tender and women tough. (Have you not seen the pictures of a little girl, armed only with a twig, shepherding contented geese to pasture?) It is not a dish the preparation of which is to be lightly undertaken, nor should the dyspeptic be asked to assist at its consumption. Wait, rather, until you are cooking for a group of men who, rising in the predawn hours, have gone duck hunting. They will return in the late morning, chilled, garrulous, and filled with the spirit of high adventure which sitting in three inches of ice water seems to engender in duck hunters. Set before them a huge bowl of steaming cassoulet with, at the right hand of each, a tumbler of white wine. Let there be crusty bread at table and, just possibly, a green salad in the background. Set, in a place apart, deep armchairs before a log fire. When you wake your guests, in time for dinner, it is probable that they will not require it.

The preparation of cassoulet involves three separate operations:

1. Secure a small-to-medium-sized goose and prick the skin all over with a skewer. Lay him-or-her on a rack in a clean pan and place in an oven at 375°. When you hear fat sizzling, turn out the oven and leave for an hour. Relight the oven, reawait the sizzling, and again turn out the oven. Repeat, twice more. The purpose of this procedure, as you will probably have gathered, is less to cook the bird than to secure the greatest possible quantity of white, unburned goose grease. Remove the bird and, while you are jointing and carving him-or-her into reasonably sized pieces, heat the goose grease until it is smoking. Place the pieces of goose in an earthenware dish and pour the hot fat over them. When cold, place in the refrigerator until required. Epicures insist that this *confit d'oie* be prepared a month in advance; but they will never find out if you make it the night before.

2. Visit your butcher and purchase from him a two-to-three-pound shoulder of mutton (or lamb). Convince him that you are stone cold sober and in your right mind, before requesting him to chop the shoulder, with a cleaver, into one-inch cubes. No, you do *not* want it boned. You just want it chopped. While he is still in shock, buy also a whole (not sliced) garlic sausage of about one-pound weight. The correct confection is the French *saucisse d'Arles* but any garlic-redolent cylinder will

serve. The acquisition of half a pound of salt pork will come as a relief to both of you.

3. Secure three pints of dried beans (the kind Bostonians bake), a gallon of white wine (California sauterne is excellent), and two or three bay leaves.

Now for the cooking. Mix the bay leaves with the beans; cover with white wine and leave to soak overnight. In the morning, raise rapidly to the boil and simmer for about an hour, making sure that the wine is always above the level of the beans. Meanwhile chop your salt pork in quarter-inch cubes and set it to fry. Throw in, when plenty of fat has been rendered, half a pound of finely chopped onions and half an ounce of chopped garlic. As soon as the onions are golden, add the mutton and stir vigorously over a high flame until all is brown. Stir this mixture into the partially cooked beans and continue to simmer for yet another hour. Now, your beans being tender, or at least approaching tenderness, is the time to add the goose. Dig each piece from its embedding grease and add to the beans, pork, and mutton. Stir vigorously and simmer until required. Broil the sausage and lay it smoking on the dish of cassoulet.

The rest of your gallon of wine? This goes, you will remember, into tumblers at the right hand of each guest.

CASSOULET DE CASTELNAUDARY
Samuel Chamberlain

Soak 2 pounds of dried white beans in tepid water for 2 hours. Drain the beans and put them in a kettle with 5 quarts of water, ½ pound of pork rind, ¼ pound of bacon or salt ham, 6 cloves of garlic, chopped, a branch of thyme, 3 tablespoons salt, and a good pinch each of pepper and mixed spices. Bring the water very gradually to a boil and simmer the beans very, very slowly for about 1½ hours, or until they are tender. Do not let them boil or the skins will break.

While the beans are cooking, grill 1 pound of fresh sausage. Cut 2 pounds of fresh pork into cubes of about 1 ounce each and brown the cubes lightly in goose fat. Dissolve the pan juices with 2 tablespoons hot water and add these juices to the beans.

When the beans are cooked, remove the pork rind and the bacon and cut into ¾-inch squares. Discard the branch of thyme.

Now you will need a *cassole* (large earthen pot) for the cassoulet. Put a third of the beans in it. In the center place a leg and second joint of preserved goose (*confit d'oie*) and around this the browned cubes of pork, the grilled sausage, and the squares of pork rind and bacon. Cover with the rest of the beans and their plentiful juices.

Place the dish in a very slow oven where it should remain 4 hours or longer. It is the oven which makes a good cassoulet. Some people sprinkle the dish with bread crumbs before putting it in the oven. In any case, the oven heat must be as low as possible, and the final dish should be quite liquid and succulent.

To this recipe we would add that the nearest equivalent to the French dried beans, which stay white in cooking—most of ours turn brown—can be purchased from Italian importers. Ask for white kidney beans. *Confit d'oie* is canned in its own fat and is imported from southern France.

The cassoulet has its drawbacks. It is not a light dish. In fact, it has star-billing in Dr. Edouard de Pomaine's volume *Twenty Dishes Which Give You the Gout*. This is a memorable cookbook with a different approach. Its twenty recipes are heartbreakingly tempting. It was prepared for the medical profession in France and was distributed free to doctors by a medicine company. And what was the medicine company selling? A medicine to cure the gout! And what are the other nineteen gout-giving divinities? Many of the most beautiful regional dishes in France, alas! Here is the complete list: *soupe aux oignons, bouillabaise, fondue au fromage, pilaf aux foies de volailles, poitrine de veau aux champignons, quiche au lard, grosse carpe cuite au four, paquets de tripes, coq au vin, cassoulet, pâté de saumon, poulet à la reine Marie, choux braisés à viande perdue, rognons flambés, meurette d'anguilles, jambon en croûts, hochepot, langouste à la crème, goulache de queue de boeuf, ragoût d'oie à l'aigre-doux.* We are compelled to confess that for the sake of these delights the gout might well be endured.

CASSOULET FROM CASTELNAUDARY
Curnonsky

1 *pound haricot beans*	1¾ *pounds preserved*
5 *onions*	*goose*
15 *cloves garlic*	6 *tomatoes*
1 *pound salt pork*	1 *pound fresh shoulder*
1 *pound knuckle of pork*	*of pork*
1 *small piece bacon rind*	5–6 *ounces garlic*
6 *ounces salami*	*sausage*
1 *carrot*	4 *country-style sausages*
3 *cloves*	*Bread crumbs*
2 *bouquets garnis*	*Salt and pepper*

Soak the beans for 8 to 10 hours the day before. Cook in a glazed earthenware pot in salted water, adding the onion, 4 cloves of garlic, the salt pork, knuckle of pork, bacon rind, salami, carrot, cloves, and a large bouquet garni (2½ to 3 hours).

Prepare a stew with the preserved goose and tomatoes, seasoning highly. Add 2 chopped onions, 5 cloves of garlic, and a bouquet garni. This stew should not be too liquid. Cook 45 minutes.

Prepare a separate stew with the shoulder of pork, adding the same ingredients as for the goose stew. Cook 3 hours.

Cook the garlic sausage separately in some of the liquid from the beans.

Fry the 4 country-style sausages.

Drain the beans and then add them to the sauce from both stews. Season to taste.

Rub a large glazed earthenware casserole with the remaining garlic and cover the bottom with a bed of beans. Lay the goose stew, pork stew, garlic sausage, and country-style sausages on top and cover with the rest of the beans. Cook on medium fire for ½ hour.

Pour fat from the sausages and stews over the bread crumbs and sprinkle on the beans. Brown in the oven.

(The meat can be prepared separately or together with the beans.)

CASSOULET DE PORC ET DE MOUTON

Beck, Bertholle, and Child

(Beans Baked with Pork Loin,
Shoulder of Mutton or Lamb, and Sausage)

For 10 to 12 people

THE PORK LOIN

2½ *pounds of boned pork loin, excess fat removed (It will taste even better if marinated overnight in salt and spices)*

Roast the pork to an internal temperature of 175 to 180°. Set it aside to cool. Reserve cooking juices.

THE BEANS

2 *pounds or 5 cups dry white beans (great northern, preferably)*

An 8-quart kettle containing 5 quarts of rapidly boiling water

Drop the beans into the boiling water. Bring rapidly back to the boil and boil for 2 minutes. Remove from heat and let the beans soak in the water for 1 hour; they will cook in the soaking water, and the cooking should proceed as soon as possible after the soaking process is completed.

½ *pound fresh pork*   *A heavy saucepan*
rind or salt pork rind   *Heavy shears*

While the beans are soaking, place the rind in the saucepan and cover with 1 quart of cold water. Bring to the boil and boil 1 minute. Drain, rinse in cold water, and repeat the process.

Then, with shears, cut the rind into strips ¼ inch wide; cut the strips into small triangles. Cover the rind again with a quart of cold water, bring to the simmer, and simmer very slowly for 30 minutes. Set saucepan aside. This process freshens the rind, and softens it so it will lose itself as it cooks with the beans.

> A 1-pound chunk of fresh, unsalted, unsmoked lean bacon (or very good quality lean salt pork simmered for 10 minutes in 2 quarts of water and drained)
> 1 cup (4 ounces) sliced onions
> The pork rind and its cooking liquid
> A large herb bouquet, with garlic and cloves: 6 to 8 parsley sprigs, 4 unpeeled cloves garlic, 2 cloves, ½ teaspoon thyme, and 2 bay leaves tied in cheesecloth
> No salt until later if you have used salt pork; otherwise 1 tablespoon salt

Place all the ingredients above in the kettle with the soaked beans. Bring to the simmer. Skin off any skum which may rise. Simmer slowly, uncovered, for about 1½ hours or until the beans are just tender. Add boiling water if necessary during cooking, to keep beans covered with liquid. Season to taste near end of cooking. Leave beans in their cooking liquid until ready to use, then drain. Reserve cooking liquid. Remove the bacon or salt pork and set aside. Discard the herb packet.

THE LAMB OR MUTTON

> 2 to 2½ pounds boned shoulder or breast of mutton or almost mature lamb, fell (skin covering meat) and excess fat removed
> 4 to 6 tablespoons rendered fresh pork fat, pork-roast drippings, goose fat or cooking oil; more if needed
> A heavy, 8-quart fireproof casserole
> About 1 pound cracked mutton or lamb bones; some pork bones may be included
> 2 cups (½ pound) minced onions

Cut the lamb or mutton into chunks roughly 2 inches square. Dry each piece in paper towels. Pour a ¹⁄₁₆-inch layer of fat into the casserole and heat until the fat is almost smoking. Brown the meat, a few pieces at a time, on all sides. Remove to a side dish. Brown the bones and add to meat. If fat has burned, replace with 3 tablespoons of fresh fat. Lower heat, brown onions lightly about 5 minutes.

4 cloves mashed garlic
6 tablespoons fresh tomato purée, tomato paste, or 4 large tomatoes peeled, seeded, and juiced
½ teaspoon thyme
2 bay leaves

3 cups dry white wine or 2 cups dry white vermouth
1 quart brown stock or 3 cups canned beef bouillon and 1 cup water
Salt and pepper

Return the bones and lamb or mutton to the casserole and stir in all ingredients on the left. Bring to simmer on top of stove, season lightly with salt. Cover and simmer slowly on top of stove or in a 325° oven for 1½ hours. Remove the meat to a dish; discard the bones and bay leaves. Remove all but 2 tablespoons fat; carefully correct seasoning of cooking liquid.

FINAL FLAVORING OF BEANS

Pour the cooked and drained beans into the lamb cooking juices. Stir in any juices you may have from the roast pork. Add bean cooking liquid, if necessary, so beans are covered. Simmer 5 minutes, then let beans stand in the liquid 10 minutes to absorb flavor. Drain beans when you are ready for final assembly.

HOMEMADE SAUSAGE CAKES
—a substitute for Saucisse de Toulouse

1 pound (2 cups) lean fresh pork
⅓ pound (⅔ cup) fresh pork fat
A meat grinder
A 3-quart mixing bowl
A wooden spoon
2 teaspoons salt
⅛ teaspoon pepper
Big pinch allspice

⅛ teaspoon crumbled bay leaf
¼ cup armagnac or cognac
A small clove mashed garlic
Optional: 1 chopped truffle and the juice from the can

Put the pork and fat through the medium blade of the meat grinder. Place in bowl and beat in the rest of the ingredients above. Sauté a small spoonful and taste for seasoning, adding more to the mixture if you feel it necessary. Form into cakes 2 inches in diameter and ½ inch thick. Brown lightly over moderate heat in a skillet. Drain on paper towels.

FINAL ASSEMBLY

An 8-quart fireproof casserole 5 to 6 inches high: brown
earthenware glazed inside is typical, but other types of
glazed pottery or enameled iron will do nicely
2 *cups dry white bread crumbs mixed with ½ cup chopped*
parsley
3 *to 4 tablespoons pork roasting fat or goose fat*

Cut the roast pork into 1½-to-2-inch serving chunks. Slice the bacon or salt pork into serving pieces ¼ inch thick. Arrange a layer of beans in the bottom of the casserole, then continue with layers of lamb or mutton, roast pork, bacon slices, sausage cakes, and beans, ending with a layer of beans and sausage cakes. Pour on the meat cooking juices, and enough bean cooking juice so liquid comes just to the top layer of beans. Spread on the crumbs and parsley, and dribble the fat on top. Set aside or refrigerate until you are ready to take up the final cooking of about an hour. The cassoulet should be served soon after its baking, so it will not dry out or overcook.

BAKING

Preheat oven to 375°. Bring the casserole to the simmer on top of the stove. Then set it in the upper third of the preheated oven. When the top has crusted lightly, in about 20 minutes, turn the oven down to 350°. Break the crust into the beans with the back of a spoon, and baste with the liquid in the casserole. Repeat several times, as the crust forms again, but leave a final crust intact for serving. If the liquid in the casserole becomes too thick during the baking period, add a spoonful or two of bean cooking liquid. The cassoulet should bake for about an hour; serve it from its casserole.

CASSOULET À LA MINNEWASSO

This recipe was inspired mainly by that of Beck, Bertholle, and Child in *Mastering the Art of French Cooking*, given above. We hope to develop a "cassoulet à la Minnelea" but must await the opportunity to work on the spot at "Minnelea," our home in Italy, using local foodstuffs. Here are the ingredients used for the dish served on January 6, 1966 (preparations started on January 4), planned for 25 people:

6 *pounds dried great northern or other white beans*	2 *pounds Polish sausage*
	8 *onions (1 pound)*
	1 *cup dry white wine*
2 *ducks (5 pounds each)*	*Bouquet garni (parsley,*
¼ *pound salt pork*	*garlic, thyme, cloves,*
10 *pounds pork loin*	*bay leaf)*
½ *leg lamb (3 pounds)*	*Salt to taste*

Our guests were extravagant in their praise and gave material evidence of their opinion by the way they demolished the cassoulet; the amount left over was barely enough for three of us the next day.

This dish is best prepared in large quantity. The portion not required at the time of preparation can be successfully frozen for future use.

The complete preparation can be done in a day, but we enjoyed the following 3-day method. On the first day, roast the ducks so that they will be ready by dinnertime, taking care that they are not too well done. Serve your family one-half duck for dinner (if your family is larger than 4 or 5, cook 3 ducks). Cut the remaining duck into bite-sized pieces, mince about half of the crisp brown skin. Discard the fat in the roaster.

On the second day, again combine preparation for the cassoulet with your dinner plans, roasting the pork to be ready for family dinner, allowing 2 pounds for the meal. The lamb can be roasted at the same time. Season the pork with ½ teaspoon thyme and the lamb with slivers of garlic inserted into the flesh.

After dinner cut the meat into bite-sized pieces. Reserve the drippings, discarding the congealed fat before adding to the cassoulet. The beans can also be cooked on the second day so that you can have your family taste them for seasoning.

To cook the beans:

Your largest kettle is probably too small to contain the 6 pounds of beans—an 8-quart kettle is fine for cooking 3 pounds. Divide the beans among such pots as you have or can borrow. In each pot cover the beans with cold water, bring slowly to a boil, then set aside to soak for an hour. Now add the salt pork, one piece in each pot, and the sliced onions. Tie the seasonings in a piece of cheesecloth—a dozen parsley sprigs, 8 to 10 cloves of garlic, 4 to 6 whole cloves, ½ teaspoon thyme, and a bay leaf and add to the bean kettle. Divide these ingredients into two parts if cooking the beans in two containers. Again bring the beans slowly to the boiling point, reduce heat and simmer until the beans are tender, 1½ to 2 hours, adding boiling water as necessary. When beans are done, remove the salt pork and bouquet garni. Taste for saltiness, adding more salt as needed. The beans should be kept in their cooking liquid until ready to be combined with the meat. Then drain them, saving the liquor, and place the beans and cut-up meats in alternate layers in one or more oven-proof dishes. Precook the Polish sausage in boiling water for 5 minutes, then slice it and top the casserole with it. Or slice and then partially cook it in a skillet, drain on paper towels, and add to the casserole. Pour wine (if desired) and bean liquid to the level of the top bean layer.

Cover casserole and cook in a 350° oven until thoroughly hot, then remove cover and bake for ½ to 1 hour, adding bean liquor if necessary. Serve in the casserole.

PER RECIPE: 22,650 cal., 2184 g. protein, 948 g. fat (320 sat., 104 poly.)
FOR 30 SERVINGS, 760 calories per serving

MOCK CASSOULET

Here is a suggestion for something like a cassoulet, much reduced in ingredients and in preparation time, for an ordinary family meal.

2½ cups (1 pound)
  great northern beans
1 clove garlic, minced
3 onions, sliced
1 tablespoon parsley
  flakes

¼ teaspoon thyme
½ pound boneless pork
  chops
1 pound bulk pork
  sausage
Salt to taste

Soak and simmer beans as described in the introduction to the chapter on SOUPS. Add garlic, onion, parsley flakes, thyme, and salt at the start of simmering.

Meanwhile brown pork chops well, then cut into bite-sized pieces, discarding fat.

Shape sausage into patties, cook slowly in skillet until nearly done. Discard drippings and drain patties on paper.

Drain beans, reserving liquor. Transfer beans and pork to shallow casserole, arrange sausage patties on top. Add enough bean liquor to just cover beans. Reserve the rest to add later, as needed. Cover the casserole and bake in a slow (250–300°) oven for ½ hour or more. This dish will wait for late-comers; just check for dryness and add more bean liquor as necessary.

PER RECIPE: 3500 cal., 196 g. protein, 164 g. fat (61 sat., 19 poly.)
FOR 6 SERVINGS, 580 calories per serving

LUNCH OR SUPPER

No real division of bean recipes can be made, designating this dish for lunch, another for dinner. It is said that in Boston they are eaten for breakfast as well. The recipes in this section are suggested for either an informal evening meal or a fairly substantial lunch, but they should not be forgotten when planning a more formal dinner or an after-the-theater buffet. They are assembled in the following groups: *Just Beans; Beans with Rice; Beans with Potatoes, Pasta, or Barley; Buffet and Snack Specials.*

I. JUST BEANS

Because beans themselves are so low in fat, they are usually cooked with fat meats, often salt pork, bacon or sausage, or animal fat in the form of lard. These recipes, both traditional and new, are without meat. Vegetable oil is used in most of them.

GERMAN BEANS

2½ cups dried navy beans (1 pound)	*1 cup bread crumbs browned in 2 tablespoons oil*
1 tablespoon flour	
3 tablespoons oil	*Salt to taste*

Soak and simmer beans as directed in the introduction to the chapter on soups. When tender, drain and pass through a sieve.

Brown flour slightly in 1 tablespoon of oil, stir it into the bean purée, then stir in the other 2 tablespoons oil. Reheat and serve with a topping of browned bread crumbs.

PER RECIPE: 2590 cal., 112 g. protein, 82 g. fat (7 sat., 38 poly.) FOR 8 SERVINGS, 320 calories per serving

KIDNEY BEAN PATTIES

1 cup dried red kidney beans	½ cup chopped chives (or shallots, parsley, or combination)
2 tablespoons oil	1 lemon

Soak and simmer beans as described in the introduction to the chapter on SOUPS. Drain beans, reserving the liquor.

Heat oil in a skillet, add chives, or shallots, or parsley, or a mixture of all three; then add beans and cook, mashing with a fork. When beans are all mashed, add liquor and continue cooking over very low heat, stirring occasionally, until water has all evaporated. Form into patties and serve with a slice of lemon.

PER RECIPE: 960 cal., 41 g. protein, 31 g. fat (4 sat., 18 poly.) FOR 4 SERVINGS, 240 calories per serving

KIDNEY BEANS WITH YOGURT

2 (1-pound) cans red kidney beans	4 green onions with tops, cut in ½-inch lengths
¼ cup dry red wine	Salt and pepper to taste
	8 ounces yogurt

Mix beans with wine and onion. Turn into a casserole and heat, seasoning with salt and pepper. Serve with the yogurt in a separate dish.

PER RECIPE: 970 cal., 60 g. protein, 7 g. fat (3 sat., 2 poly.) FOR 6 SERVINGS, 160 calories per serving

INDIAN CHICK-PEAS

Chick-peas, or garbanzos, are called Bengal gram in India, where they are eaten in great quantities and prepared in many ways.

1 pound chick-peas
2 onions, sliced
4 tablespoons oil
1½ teaspoons turmeric
¾ tablespoon fresh
    ginger root, or
¼ teaspoon powdered
    ginger

6 mint leaves
½ teaspoon chili powder
2 tomatoes
Salt to taste
1 lemon

Soak, then simmer chick-peas until tender as directed for beans in the introduction to the chapter on SOUPS. Drain and reserve the stock. Cook onion in oil, adding turmeric, ginger root or ginger, mint leaves, and chick-peas, then chili and tomatoes. Cook 10 to 12 minutes; add salt. Stock can be added if a more liquid dish is desired. Add the juice of a lemon or serve with lemon slices.

PER RECIPE: 2310 cal., 100 g. protein, 79 g. fat (8 sat., 41 poly.) FOR 6 SERVINGS, 390 calories per serving

SPICED LENTILS

1½ cups lentils
2 tablespoons oil
2 tablespoons flour
2 small onions, chopped
¼ teaspoon powdered
    ginger, or

1 tablespoon minced
    ginger root if available
½ teaspoon chili
    powder
Juice of ½ lemon
Salt and paprika to taste

Soak and simmer lentils as described for beans in the introduction to the chapter on SOUPS. Continue to cook until lentils are tender, from 1 to 2 hours. Drain, reserving the liquor.

Cook the onion in the oil for 5 minutes, stir in the flour, and add 1 cup of lentil liquor, cook and stir over moderate heat until boiling. Combine drained lentils with this sauce. Season with ginger, chili powder, lemon juice, and salt and paprika. Place in oven-proof dish and keep hot in 300° oven until ready to serve.

PER RECIPE: 1340 cal., 70 g. protein, 32 g. fat (3 sat., 16 poly.)
FOR 4 SERVINGS, 340 calories per serving

CABBAGE AND CHICK-PEAS

1 pound chick-peas
¼ pound cabbage, chopped
1 clove garlic, minced
½ pound pumpkin or yellow squash, peeled and cubed

1 small onion, sliced
1 tomato, cubed
½ green pepper, chopped
1 tablespoon olive oil
1 teaspoon vinegar
½ cup tomato sauce
2 teaspoons salt

Soak chick-peas overnight. Drain. Add 2½ quarts of water and bring to a boil. Add cabbage, garlic, pumpkin or squash, onion, tomato, and green pepper and simmer for 1½ hours. Add olive oil, vinegar, tomato sauce, and salt and cook for another ½ hour.

PER RECIPE: 1810 cal., 101 g. protein, 23 g. fat (trace sat., 10 poly.)
FOR 6 SERVINGS, 300 calories per serving

LATIN-AMERICAN BLACK BEANS

This dish is popular in Brazil, in Cuba, and in Puerto Rico, and elsewhere in Latin America. It is usually served with rice, and in Puerto Rico the beans and rice are often cooked together.

4 cups (2 pounds) black beans
1 large onion, chopped
1 clove garlic, chopped

⅓ cup oil
1½ teaspoons salt
¼ teaspoon pepper

Soak and simmer beans as directed in the introduction to the chapter on SOUPS, until beans are tender but still retain their shape, for about 2 hours. Fry onion and garlic in oil in a skillet until lightly browned. Drain 2 cups of cooked beans and allow the rest to remain in their liquid. Cook the drained beans with the onion and garlic; season with salt and pepper and stir well until they have absorbed the oil. Then return to moist beans, adjust seasoning, simmer gently for about 10 minutes, and serve.

PER RECIPE: 3830 cal., 205 g. protein, 89 g. fat (8 sat., 46 poly.) FOR 8 SERVINGS, 480 calories per serving

NUT LOAF

2 cups soft bread crumbs
1½ cups chopped
    peanuts
1 cup cooked rice

1 egg
¾ cup skim milk
Salt and pepper to taste

Combine all ingredients, place in oiled loaf pan. Bake in moderate (350°) oven for 30 minutes. Serve with chili sauce.

PER RECIPE: 1860 cal., 86 g. protein, 105 g. fat (24 sat., 29 poly.) FOR 6 SERVINGS, 310 calories per serving

QUICK TAMALE PIE

2 cups cornmeal
2 teaspoons salt
2 (1-pound) cans (4
    cups) chili con carne
    with beans

12 ripe olives (optional)
or
2 pimentos (optional)

Cook cornmeal according to directions on package for corn-meal mush. When done, line bottom and sides of a 2-quart oiled casserole with ⅔ of the mixture, saving ⅓ for the top crust. Add chili. Spread remaining crust mixture over the top. Garnish with sliced ripe olives or strips of pimento if desired. Bake in hot (400°) oven for 25 to 30 minutes.

PER RECIPE: 2410 cal., 93 g. protein, 73 g. fat (29 sat., 4 poly.) FOR 6 SERVINGS, 400 calories per serving

BEAN LOAF, BAKED

¼ *cup minced onion*
¼ *cup minced green*
   pepper
2 *tablespoons oil*
4 *cups mashed baked*
   beans

2 *eggs, slightly beaten*
2 *cups bread crumbs*
1 *cup cooked or canned*
   tomatoes
½ *teaspoon paprika*
Salt and pepper to taste

Cook onion and pepper in oil until the onion is transparent, about 10 minutes. Add to the beans. Then add, in succession, eggs, bread crumbs, and tomatoes. Season with paprika, salt and pepper. Transfer to an oiled loaf pan and bake at 350° for ½ hour. Serve with tomato sauce.

PER RECIPE: 2270 cal., 102 g. protein, 53 g. fat (9 sat., 20 poly.) FOR 6 SERVINGS, 380 calories per serving

BOILED BEANS WITH CURRY SAUCE

1 *onion, chopped*
2 *tablespoons oil*
1 *teaspoon salt*
2 *tablespoons flour*
2 *tablespoons curry*
   powder
1 *clove garlic, minced*

2 *cups stock*
1 *apple*
½ *cup chopped dates*
Juice of ½ lemon
4 *cups cooked kidney or*
   other beans

Cook onion in oil until golden, add salt, flour, curry powder, and garlic, and blend well. Add stock and cook, stirring constantly until thick. Peel the apple, cut it into eight pieces, and add it to the sauce with the dates, lemon juice, and beans. Heat thoroughly and serve.

PER RECIPE: 1180 cal., 41 g. protein, 32 g. fat (2 sat., 15 poly.) FOF 4 SERVINGS, 300 calories per serving

GARDEN CHILI

2 onions, chopped
3 stalks celery, sliced
2 green peppers, chopped
2 tablespoons oil
1 (15-oz.) can chili hot
    beans

4 small tomatoes,
    quartered
Salt to taste
Chili powder to taste

Cook onion, celery, and peppers in oil for 5 minutes. Add
beans and tomatoes, and salt and chili powder if desired. Heat
thoroughly and serve with rice.

PER RECIPE: 1060 cal., 43 g. protein, 32 g. fat (2 sat., 16 poly.)
FOR 4 SERVINGS, 270 calories per serving

II. BEANS WITH RICE

Beans and rice have long made a favorite combination in many
countries, and modern nutritionists have found that the nutritional result is excellent. Neither beans nor rice alone provide
an ideal assortment of amino acids to make the highest-quality
protein, but what is short in each of these foodstuffs is made up
in the combination. In general, beans and their relatives together
with cereals do a fine job. Many good bean and rice combinations have been developed in India and in China, but Central
and South America and even Europe contribute good recipes for
rice combined with peas, lentils, bean sprouts, and peanuts as
well as with beans.

CURRIED BROWN BEANS WITH RICE

1 cup dried brown (or
    other) beans
2 onions, chopped
2 tablespoons oil

1 tablespoon curry
    powder
1 teaspoon salt

Soak and simmer beans according to directions in the introduction to the chapter on SOUPS. Drain the beans, reserving liquor.

Cook onion in oil until transparent, add curry powder, salt, drained beans, and ½ cup bean liquor. Simmer 15 minutes.

Serve with steaming hot rice. A good accompanying dish can be made as follows:

Core but do not peel 3 or 4 apples. Slice and cook them in 1 tablespoon oil with a few paper-thin slices of unpeeled lemon and ½ cup raisins.

PER RECIPE: 1070 cal., 57 g. protein, 32 g. fat (3 sat., 16 poly.) FOR 4 SERVINGS, 270 calories per serving

PEAS AND CARROTS WITH CURRIED RICE

1 small onion, sliced
3 tablespoons oil
1 cup rice
1 to 2 tablespoons curry
   powder
2 cups broth
Salt and freshly ground
   black pepper to taste

Juice of ½ lemon
6 medium-sized carrots,
   sliced
3 cups shelled peas
   (3 pounds in shell),
or
2 packages frozen peas

Fry onion in 2 tablespoons oil until transparent. Add rice and curry powder, stir well. Add broth, salt and pepper, and lemon juice. Bring to boil, reduce heat, and simmer until rice is tender and liquid absorbed, about 20 minutes.

Meanwhile cook carrots in minimum amount of salted water until half tender, about 10 minutes; add peas and cook 10 to 20 minutes longer, until peas are done. Spoon rice in ring around warmed serving platter. Fill center with peas and carrots.

PER RECIPE: 1610 cal., 52 g. protein, 45 g. fat (3 sat., 22 poly.) FOR 6 SERVINGS, 270 calories per serving

LENTILS AND PEPPER-RICE

1 cup lentils
Salt and pepper
(cayenne or red pepper
pod)
2 large onions, sliced

1 tablespoon oil
1 large tomato, diced
1 cup rice
2 cups stock or stock
substitute

Soak, then simmer lentils until tender, about 3 hours in all. Season with salt and pepper. Fry onion in oil until soft but not brown. Add diced tomato, rice, and stock or stock substitute. Cover tightly and simmer until rice is tender. Fold in drained lentils; correct the seasoning.

PER RECIPE: 1500 cal., 66 g. protein, 4 g. fat (1 sat., 2 poly.)
FOR 6 SERVINGS, 250 calories per serving

HAITI PLATE NATIONAL

1 cup dried kidney beans
1½ teaspoons salt
1 onion
1 clove garlic
3 sprigs parsley

2 tablespoons oil
½ teaspoon pepper
¼ teaspoon ground
cloves
1 cup raw rice

Pick over and wash the beans, put in kettle with 1 quart of water, boil 5 minutes, remove from heat, add salt, and allow to soak for 1 hour.

Meanwhile chop onion, garlic, and parsley; sauté in 1 tablespoon of the oil; add pepper and cloves. Remove to casserole.

Drain the beans, reserving liquor. Add the remaining tablespoon of oil to that in the skillet and sauté beans for 5 minutes over medium heat. Add beans to casserole. Measure bean liquor and add enough boiling water to make 5½ cups. Pour over beans, cover casserole, and bake in 250° oven for 2 hours or until beans begin to soften. Stir in raw rice and bake 1 hour longer, adding water if needed.

PER RECIPE: 1620 cal., 57 g. protein, 32 g. fat (5 sat., 18 poly.)
FOR 8 SERVINGS, 200 calories per serving

RICE AND BEAN SPROUTS

This recipe comes from Korea.

2 cups rice
1 green onion, chopped
1 clove garlic, minced
2 teaspoons prepared
 sesame seeds (see
 below)

2 tablespoons soy sauce
1 teaspoon oil
1 cup prepared bean
 sprouts

Wash rice well and add 3 cups cold water. Combine onion, garlic, sesame seeds, soy sauce, oil, and bean sprouts; cook all together for 2 minutes, stirring well. Combine bean sprout mixture and rice, cover tightly, and bring quickly to a boil. Reduce heat as low as possible and steam 30 minutes. Do not stir or remove the lid while cooking.

PREPARED SESAME SEEDS:

1 cup sesame seeds   1 teaspoon salt

Put seeds in a heavy skillet and brown slowly, stirring constantly. When the seeds are brown and rounded, remove at once from the fire. Add salt. Mash the seeds until pulverized.

PER RECIPE: 1500 cal., 33 g. protein, 9 g. fat (1 sat., 2 poly.)
FOR 6 SERVINGS, 250 calories per serving

PEANUTS, CELERY, AND RICE

1 cup rice
1 cup sliced celery
2 green onions with
 tops, chopped

3 tablespoons oil
½ cup chopped salted
 peanuts
Additional salt to taste

Boil rice your usual method. Meanwhile cook celery and onion in oil for about 5 minutes. Mix with rice before serving.

PER RECIPE: 1600 cal., 34 g. protein, 79 g. fat (11 sat., 31 poly.)
FOR 4 SERVINGS, 400 calories per serving

GREEN AND RED RICE

A sophisticated "Hoppin' John."

1 egg	½ cup chopped parsley
1 cup skim milk	1 small onion
1 (15½-oz.) can	1 teaspoon salt
kidney beans	2 cups cooked rice
1 clove garlic	¼ cup grated cheese

Beat egg until light; add milk. Drain kidney beans. Combine all ingredients and put in oiled baking dish. Bake in 350° oven for ½ hour.

PER RECIPE: 1110 cal., 58 g. protein, 17 g. fat (7 sat., 1 poly.)
FOR 4 SERVINGS, 280 calories per serving

SHRIMPS, PEAS, AND RICE

2 onions, sliced	Salt and pepper to taste
2 stalks celery, thinly	2 cups boiled shelled
sliced	shrimps
2 tablespoons oil	1 cup raw rice
2 cups fresh shelled peas	½ teaspoon sweet basil
1 no. 2 can solid-pack	
tomatoes	

Cook onion and celery in oil in a heavy saucepan for about 10 minutes; add peas, tomatoes, and salt and pepper and cook slowly until peas are done (10 to 15 minutes). Add shrimps and basil and continue to cook only until shrimps are hot.

Cook rice in 2 cups of water in heavy pan, covered, over low heat or in top of double boiler over slowly boiling water for 20 to 25 minutes or until rice is tender and all water is absorbed. Combine with shrimp mixture and serve very hot.

PER RECIPE: 1670 cal., 106 g. protein, 35 g. fat (2 sat., 15 poly.)
FOR 6 SERVINGS, 280 calories per serving

PEAS AND RICE PROVENÇALE

¼ cup chopped onion
4 tablespoons salad oil
½ clove garlic, finely
  chopped
½ cup sliced green
  olives

2 cups cooked peas
2 cups hot cooked rice
Pimento strips
¼ cup chopped parsley

Sauté onion in oil until tender, about 10 minutes; add garlic and olives and cook 1 minute longer. Combine with peas and rice; toss gently. Garnish with pimento strips and parsley.

PER RECIPE: 1250 cal., 26 g. protein, 69 g. fat (5 sat., 30 poly.) FOR 6 SERVINGS, 210 calories per serving

III. BEANS WITH POTATOES, PASTA, OR BARLEY

The combination of beans with potatoes or with macaroni needs only the addition of a green leafy vegetable or salad to make a nutritionally complete meal.

BEANS AND ELBOW MACARONI

1 cup dried navy beans
1 cup "creamettes,"
  elbow macaroni, or the
  like
1 (1-pound) can
  tomatoes
2 cloves garlic

Salt and freshly ground
  pepper to taste
1 teaspoon beef stock
  base, Ac'cent, or
  monosodium glutamate
½ teaspoon
  Worchestershire sauce

Soak and simmer beans according to directions in the introduction to the chapter on SOUPS. Drain the beans. Cook "creamettes" according to directions on the package. Combine beans, creamettes, and tomatoes with seasonings. Simmer 20 to 30 minutes until flavors are well blended and the liquid of the tomatoes is somewhat reduced.

PER RECIPE: 1330 cal., 70 g. protein, 6 g. fat (1 sat., 4 poly.) FOR 4 SERVINGS, 330 calories per serving

LENTILS, NUTS, AND NOODLES

1 *pound lentils*
12 *ounces noodles*
Salt and pepper to taste
2 *large onions, cut into*
   thin slices

2 *tablespoons oil*
½ *cup Spanish peanuts*
   or chopped filberts or
   hazelnuts

Soak and simmer lentils as described for beans in the introduction to the chapter on soups, using the minimum amount of water. Season with salt and pepper and cook until the lentils are tender, about 2 hours. When the lentils are done, allow them to continue simmering while cooking the noodles according to the directions on the package. Fry onion slices in oil until golden, then stir in the nuts.

Place the drained noodles on a heated platter, pour the lentils over them, and top with the onion-nut mixture.

PER RECIPE: 3660 cal., 178 g. protein, 85 g. fat (14 sat., 28 poly.) FOR 10 SERVINGS, 370 calories per serving

LIMA BEANS AND RICED POTATOES

2 *cups cooked lima*
   beans
2 *cups riced potatoes*

1 *tablespoon oil*
½ *cup hot milk*
Salt and pepper to taste

Purée lima beans. Mix all ingredients and beat until creamy. Pile into oiled baking dish and bake in hot (425°) oven until top is brown. Serve from baking dish.

PER RECIPE: 840 cal., 38 g. protein, 16 g. fat (1 sat., 8 poly.) FOR 4 SERVINGS, 210 calories per serving

BEAN AND POTATO CAKES

2 *to* 3 *medium-sized*
   potatoes
Salt and pepper to taste

1 *cup cooked drained*
   navy or other beans
2 *tablespoons oil*

Peel potatoes and cut into small pieces, bring to boil in minimum amount of water, seasoning with salt and pepper, then turn heat down and simmer until done. There should be only 1 to 2 tablespoons of water left; if there is more, pour off all but 1 tablespoon. Beat potato with a fork, not attempting to mash completely. Add beans, mix well, shape into cakes, and brown on both sides in oil in heavy skillet.

PER RECIPE: 720 cal., 21 g. protein, 29 g. fat (2 sat., 14 poly.) FOR 4 SERVINGS, 180 calories per serving

STRING BEANS WITH SHRIMPS

1 clove garlic
2 tablespoons oil
1 cup fresh shrimps
 (⅓ pound) or frozen
 shrimps

1 small onion, sliced
2 medium-sized tomatoes,
 cut into 8 sections
1 pound green beans
1 teaspoon salt

Peel and mash the garlic. Heat it in the hot oil, then discard it. Clean the shrimps and cut in two. Fry them in oil with the onion until they begin to brown, then add the tomatoes. Break beans into 1½-inch pieces. Add them to the mixture with ¾ cup water and 1 teaspoon salt, cover and cook until the beans are tender, for 15 to 20 minutes.

PER RECIPE: 730 cal., 52 g. protein, 32 g. fat (3 sat., 15 poly.) FOR 6 SERVINGS, 120 calories per serving

SOUTHERN POT-ROASTED GREEN BEANS

1 pound green beans
½ ounce lean salt pork
1 clove garlic

12 tiny new potatoes
Salt and pepper to taste

Cut green beans in 1-inch lengths and cook in Dutch oven or other heavy kettle with a minimum of water, the salt pork, and garlic for about ½ hour. Peel new potatoes, put them on top of the beans, add salt and pepper, recover pot, and cook until potatoes are done—from 15 to 30 minutes.

PER RECIPE: 540 cal., 17 g. protein, 13 g. fat (5 sat., 1 poly.) FOR 4 SERVINGS, 140 calories per serving

BEANS AND CABBAGE HOT POT

1 *pound dried white beans*	2 *onions, chopped*
1 *large cabbage,*	1 *carrot, diced*
quartered	1 *turnip, diced*
1 *ham bone*	*Salt and freshly ground*
6 *large potatoes, peeled*	*pepper to taste*

Soak and simmer beans as described in the introduction to the chapter on SOUPS.

Meanwhile, in a separate kettle simmer the cabbage with the ham bone, potatoes, onion, carrot, and turnip in a minimum of water. When the beans are tender, drain and combine with the ingredients in the second kettle. Season with salt and pepper.

PER RECIPE: 2810 cal., 167 g. protein, 30 g. fat (8 sat., 7 poly.) FOR 6 SERVINGS, 470 calories per serving

PEAS AND BARLEY

1 *cup yellow split peas*	½ *teaspoon salt*
or lentils	2 *tablespoons oil*
½ *cup barley*	1 *small onion, sliced*

Soak peas or lentils and barley separately overnight. Put barley to cook in salted water to cover. After ½ hour add peas and cook together for another hour. Fry the onion in oil and add to the pea-barley mixture just before serving.

PER RECIPE: 1280 cal., 55 g. protein, 31 g. fat (3 sat., 6 poly.) FOR 4 SERVINGS, 320 calories per serving

IV. BUFFET AND SNACK SPECIALS

These are quick and easy to prepare. Try this chip dip while you are putting the finishing touches on the dinner.

CHILI CHIP DIP

1 (15½-oz.) can chili hot beans
A few drops of Tabasco sauce, if desired

Blend chili hot beans in a blender until smooth. Add Tabasco sauce. Heat over boiling water in double boiler. Serve hot with corn chips.

PER RECIPE: 390 cal., 26 g. protein, 2 g. fat (trace sat., 1 poly.)

CHICKEN GIBLETS AND LIMA BEANS

¼ pound chicken
*   giblets*
1 package frozen lima
*   beans*
2 medium-sized onions,
*   sliced*

2 tablespoons oil
2 cups cooked rice
Salt and freshly ground
*   pepper to taste*

Cook giblets in salted water until tender. The liver will be done in 10 minutes and can be removed; cook the gizzard and heart about ½ hour longer. Remove membrane from gizzards. Cook lima beans as directed on package. Cook onion in oil in a large skillet until transparent, about 10 minutes; add drained lima beans, giblets, and rice, season with salt and pepper, and keep over heat until thoroughly hot, adding some of the broth in which the giblets were cooked if mixture becomes too dry.

PER RECIPE: 1180 cal., 48 g. protein, 35 g. fat (4 sat., 16 poly.)
FOR 4 SERVINGS, 300 calories per serving

CHAFING DISH GARBANZOS

2 onions, chopped
1 green pepper, chopped
  coarsely
3 tablespoons oil
1 clove garlic, minced
⅓ pound cooked ham,
  cubed

1 (7½-oz.) can peeled
  solid-pack tomatoes
2 (15-oz.) cans
  garbanzos (chick-peas)
Salt to taste
Pinch oregano

Add onion and pepper to oil in chafing dish. Cook, stirring occasionally until onion is transparent, for about 10 minutes. Add garlic, ham, tomatoes, and drained garbanzos, season with salt and oregano, simmer for 15 minutes, stirring occasionally. This will keep well over low heat for second helpings or late guests.

PER RECIPE: 2110 cal., 112 g. protein, 75 g. fat (12 sat., 34 poly.) FOR 6 SERVINGS, 350 calories per serving

CHINESE BEAN SPROUT OMELET

2 strips bacon, diced
1 pound raw shrimps
½ cup chopped onion
2 cups bean sprouts

6 eggs
¼ cup oil
Soy sauce to taste

Cook bacon until golden brown. Remove from pan, drain on paper, then place in mixing bowl.

Clean and dice shrimp and cook in same pan. When done, in 2 to 3 minutes, place in mixing bowl with bacon. Cook onion for 5 minutes in same pan. When tender add it to ingredients in the mixing bowl. Add drained bean sprouts and unbeaten eggs; mix all together.

Put ¼ cup oil in 10-inch preheated frying pan. Dip omelet mixture by large spoonfuls into heated pan; cook over moderate heat until golden brown on one side, about 3 minutes. Turn and brown on other side. Place on hot platter and sprinkle with soy sauce.

PER RECIPE: 1550 cal., 129 g. protein, 102 g. fat (19 sat., 30 poly.) FOR 6 SERVINGS, 260 calories per serving

BEEF AND PEANUTS*

½ pound lean beef, diced
2 teaspoons oil
3 cups chopped celery
1 cup minced onions

Pepper to taste
2 tablespoons soy sauce
2 cups salted Spanish peanuts
Salt, if needed

Brown the meat in oil. Add celery, onion, pepper, soy sauce, and 1 cup water. Cover tightly and simmer 30 to 45 minutes. Add peanuts. Salt to taste. Serve with noodles or rice.

PER RECIPE: 2140 cal., 130 g. protein, 152 g. fat (36 sat., 43 poly.) FOR 6 SERVINGS, 350 calories per serving

CHILI—TEEN-AGE SPECIAL

4 medium-sized onions
½ pound ground beef
2 teaspoons salt
½ teaspoon pepper or to taste
1 tablespoon chili powder, or to taste

2 (17-oz.) cans kidney beans
1 (28-oz.) can tomatoes
4 stalks celery, chopped (optional)

Peel and slice onions. Preheat a 12-inch skillet. When it is hot, put in the onion, ground beef, salt, pepper, and chili pow-

* Adapted from Peanut Land's Shanghai Special

der; stir and cook for 5 minutes over high heat, add kidney
beans and tomatoes (and celery, if used); turn heat low and simmer for ½ hour or longer, stirring occasionally. Serve in bowls.

PER RECIPE: 1940 cal., 117 g. protein, 31 g. fat (10 sat., 4 poly.)
FOR 6 SERVINGS, 320 calories per serving

FIVE-MINUTE FIND

This was discovered when guests invited for Sunday tea stayed
for supper, and the cupboard was all but bare.

2 (15-oz.) cans garbanzos
1 cup spaghetti sauce, or
1 cup tomato sauce seasoned with:
  1 tablespoon dehydrated onion
  1 tablespoon parsley flakes
  1 clove garlic, minced
  ½ teaspoon salt
  ¼ teaspoon oregano

Drain garbanzos, mix with sauce, and heat.

PER RECIPE: 1440 cal., 81 g. protein, 19 g. fat (4 sat., 11 poly.)
FOR 4 SERVINGS, 370 calories per serving

MIXED BEANS PARMIGIANA

1 package frozen cut
green beans
1 package frozen wax
beans
1 package frozen lima
beans

1 can cream of celery
soup, diluted with ½
cup skim milk
Salt and pepper to taste
¼ cup grated
Parmesan cheese

Cook beans separately according to package directions. Drain
and mix. Place in casserole with diluted soup. Season with salt

and pepper. Sprinkle Parmesan cheese on top and bake uncovered in 350° oven until thoroughly hot, about 15 minutes.

PER RECIPE: 1000 cal., 52 g. protein, 37 g. fat (6 sat., 14 poly.) FOR 6 SERVINGS, 170 calories per serving

QUICK-BAKED BEANS

1 (1-pound) can
oven-style baked beans,
without tomato sauce
¼ cup dark brown sugar

½ teaspoon dry mustard
4 slices bacon, partially
cooked

Spread 1-inch layer of beans in baking dish, sprinkle with a little of the brown sugar and mustard. Repeat until all ingredients are used. Arrange bacon on top, bake uncovered in 375° oven for about 15 minutes.

PER RECIPE: 930 cal., 37 g. protein, 20 g. fat (7 sat., 4 poly.) FOR 3 SERVINGS, 310 calories per serving

Or try this version from a Washington, D.C., hostess:

BEANS HAWAIIAN

1 large (1-lb., 15-oz.)
can baked beans
2 onions, sliced
¼ cup dark molasses

¼ cup chili sauce
1 large (1-lb., 14-oz.)
can pineapple rings

Combine beans, onion, molasses, and chili sauce and spread in shallow oven-proof dish. Top with slices of pineapple and heat in 300° oven until thoroughly hot.

PER RECIPE: 1840 cal., 57 g. protein, 28 g. fat (8 sat., 2 poly.) FOR 6 SERVINGS, 310 calories per serving

TANGY BEAN AND BACON OPEN-FACE SANDWICH

1 small (½-pound) can
or jar baked beans
¼ cup grated American
cheese
¼ cup "hot" catsup or
ordinary catsup and a
little Tabasco sauce

1 teaspoon lemon juice
1 tablespoon chopped
parsley
½ teaspoon salt
4 slices rye bread
4 slices bacon, partially
cooked

Combine beans, cheese, catsup, lemon juice, and parsley. Season with salt. Spread on bread and top with bacon. Broil in oven for 2 minutes or until bacon is crisp.

PER RECIPE: 860 cal., 34 g. protein, 33 g. fat (12 sat., 6 poly.)
FOR 4 SERVINGS, 220 calories per serving

FAGIOLI ALL'UCCELLETTO
(Beans with Poultry Seasoning)

We had complaints from several of our Italian friends because we had omitted this favorite from the first edition.

1 pound dried white beans
¼ cup olive oil
¼ to ½ teaspoon thyme
or sage

1 clove garlic, minced
salt and pepper to taste

Soak and simmer beans as directed in the introduction to the chapter on soups, then drain them. Add garlic and thyme or sage to oil in a flameproof dish; bring to a boil, then add the beans and salt and pepper. Some recipes call for a few tablespoons of freshly strained tomato to be added at this time and cooked to dryness. Cover the dish and keep over very low heat for 5 to 10 minutes, until the beans have acquired the flavor of the seasonings.

PER RECIPE: 2072 cal., 101 g. protein, 67 g. fat (10 sat., 5 poly.)
FOR 8 SERVINGS: 259 calories per serving

DINNER

There is no uniform pattern of meals in the United States at present. There are still those who cling to the custom of a substantial meal in the middle of the day, but in general lunch is a comparatively light meal while the evening meal can be anything from a four- or five-course dinner to a frozen TV plate. Those who do not work regular daytime hours must adjust their eating habits to their occupations, and even the activities of our school children influence our mealtimes. One notable virtue of casseroles of dried beans is that they can be kept warm for hours, if necessary, or can be reheated without loss of flavor or texture.

The recipes assembled in this chapter may, of course, be eaten at any time, but they were selected as suitable for the main meal of the day.

I. BEANS WITHOUT MEAT

PREYBRANATZ

This is a Serbian specialty ordered a day ahead at the restaurant "Vinogradi." The restaurant, half an hour by car upriver from Belgrade, is set on a vine-covered slope overlooking the Danube. The preybranatz was served as a first course with cheese, green olives, and corn bread. We thought this, with a simple salad and some fruit to come, would be enough for the whole meal, especially when we were served large helpings and seconds were pressed on us. But there were five more courses to come! Here is the recipe given to us by the manager and the head chef, who came in to take a bow:

½ kilogram onion,   1 bay leaf
  browned in oil   Salt and ground
1 kilogram beans, soaked   paprika to taste
  and boiled

Here is the way we make it in the United States:

1 pound great northern   3 tablespoons oil
  or other white beans   1 bay leaf
4 or 5 medium-sized   1 teaspoon paprika (or
  onions (1 pound),   more)
  sliced   Salt to taste

Soak and simmer beans as directed in the introduction to the chapter on soups. Drain, reserving liquor. Place beans in oven-proof dish or bean pot. Meanwhile cook onion in oil until golden. Add it to the beans with salt, bay leaf, and paprika. Add enough bean liquor to almost cover beans, cover the dish, and bake in slow (250°) oven for 2 hours or longer, adding liquid as necessary.

PER RECIPE: 2070 cal., 107 g. protein, 50 g. fat (4 sat., 25 poly.) FOR 8 SERVINGS, 260 calories per serving

LIMA BEAN SOUFFLÉ

This dish cannot be kept waiting for late-comers; it should be served as soon as done.

3 tablespoons oil   1 cup cooked Fordhook
3 tablespoons flour   lima beans
1 cup milk   4 eggs, separated
Salt and pepper to taste

Make a white sauce with the oil, flour, and milk. Season the limas to taste and put in blender. Blend for 30 seconds. Add egg yolks and blend 20 seconds more. Beat egg whites until stiff but not dry. Fold into lima bean mixture. Pour into a 1-quart casserole and bake in a 325° oven for 35 to 40 minutes. Serve with the following sauce.

SAUCE FOR SOUFFLÉ:

½ cup chopped onion
3 tablespoons salad oil
1 cup peeled and seeded
  tomatoes
½ teaspoon celery salt
2 teaspoons
  Worcestershire sauce

½ teaspoon garlic salt
1 tablespoon meat glaze
½ cup ripe or green
  olives, coarsely
  chopped
2 tablespoons brandy

Sauté onion lightly in oil, add tomatoes, and simmer 10 minutes. Add all other ingredients except brandy, which should be added just before serving.

PER RECIPE: 1760 cal., 55 g. protein, 120 g. fat (15 sat., 45 poly.)
FOR 4 SERVINGS, 440 calories per serving

II. BEANS AND BEEF

BEEF STEW WITH BEANS

1 pound lean beef
2 tablespoons oil
2 large onions, coarsely
  chopped
1 tablespoon soy sauce

1 cup beef broth
4 cups cooked and
  drained navy beans
Salt to taste

Cut beef into bite-sized pieces and brown in oil in a heavy skillet with onion. Season with soy sauce, add broth, cover, and simmer until beef is tender, for about 2 hours. Add beans for last ½ hour of cooking, adding more liquid if necessary. Taste before serving and add salt if desired. For a spicier version, add ½ teaspoon rosemary, 1 tablespoon celery seed, and ¼ cup hot tomato sauce.

PER RECIPE: 2240 cal., 168 g. protein, 55 g. fat (14 sat., 17 poly.)
FOR 4 SERVINGS, 560 calories per serving

CHILI POT ROAST

1 large onion, minced
2 tablespoons oil
1 (3-pound) pot roast
2 tablespoons flour
1 teaspoon salt or to
  taste
1 tablespoon chili
  powder

1 teaspoon dried celery
leaves
1 (10½-oz.) can
condensed tomato
soup
½ teaspoon dry mustard
1½ cups dried lima
beans, soaked overnight

Sauté onion in oil until soft. Remove onion and set aside. Dredge meat with flour; sprinkle with salt, chili powder, and celery leaves. Brown in the same oil. Add soup, mustard, and cooked onion. Cover and simmer 1 hour. Add lima beans and 1 cup of the water in which they soaked. Simmer until meat and limas are tender, about 1 hour.

PER RECIPE: 3470 cal., 359 g. protein, 112 g. fat (41 sat., 23 poly.)
FOR 10 SERVINGS, 350 calories per serving

LIMA BEANS AND DRIED BEEF

1 pound dried lima
  beans
4 carrots
1 onion
1 tablespoon oil

1 (4-oz.) package dried
beef
2 tablespoons flour
1 teaspoon salt

Soak and simmer beans as described in the introduction to the chapter on SOUPS. Drain, reserving liquor, and put beans in a casserole.

Slice carrots and onion, and cook in oil until onion is golden. Tear dried beef into small pieces and add to carrot-onion mixture and cook 2 minutes longer. Add flour and salt, blend into mixture, then add 1 cup reserved liquor, and continue to cook and stir until thick. Pour this over the beans and add enough of the bean liquor to just cover beans. Cover casserole and bake in slow (250°) oven for 2 hours or longer, adding more liquid as necessary.

PER RECIPE: 2060 cal., 139 g. protein, 28 g. fat (7 sat., 13 poly.) FOR 8 SERVINGS, 250 calories per serving

CHINESE BEEF AND BEAN SPROUTS

1 pound flank or round
steak, fat removed
4 tablespoons oil
2 teaspoons salt
Dash pepper
¼ cup chopped onion
1 clove garlic, minced
1 green pepper, diced

3 cups bean sprouts
1 cup beef stock or
stock substitute
1 teaspoon powdered
ginger
2 tablespoons soy sauce
2 tablespoons cornstarch

Cut steak into thin diagonal slices. Put oil, salt, and pepper in a preheated skillet, add meat, and cook over high heat until brown. Add onion and garlic; cook for a few minutes, stirring constantly. Add green pepper, sprouts, and stock. Cover pan and simmer for 10 minutes. Blend together the ginger, soy sauce, cornstarch, and ¼ cup water, and add to the skillet; cook and stir until juice thickens. Serve immediately with hot boiled rice.

PER RECIPE: 1320 cal., 113 g. protein, 83 g. fat (16 sat., 29 poly.) FOR 4 SERVINGS, 330 calories per serving

BEEF AND BEANS WITH GREEN PEPPER

This is a very pretty dish, especially if the peppers are not cooked so long that they lose their bright green color.

½ pound cooked lean
beef (leftover roast,
pot roast, steak, etc.)
2 large green peppers
1 (15½-oz.) can kidney
beans

1 (10½-oz.) can cream
of celery soup
1 teaspoon salt, or to
taste
Whiff of marjoram

Cut leftover beef into ½-inch cubes. Remove seeds from pepper and cut into 1-inch pieces. Drain liquid from kidney beans. In a large saucepan or skillet dilute celery soup with ⅓ soup can of water, stir until well blended, add all other ingredients, and simmer 15 to 20 minutes, until the peppers are done to your taste.

PER RECIPE: 1020 cal., 100 g. protein, 25 g. fat (7 sat., 1 poly.) FOR 4 SERVINGS, 260 calories per serving

III. BEANS AND CHICKEN

CHICKEN AND CHICK-PEAS

3 tablespoons oil
4 chicken breasts (1 pound)
Salt to taste

1 (15-oz.) can garbanzos or chick-peas or 2 cups cooked chick-peas
2 slices Canadian bacon or 2 ounces ham, cut into small bits

Preheat a heavy skillet, add oil, and brown the chicken breasts on both sides; season with salt to taste. Add drained chick-peas and Canadian bacon or ham, reduce heat, cover pan, and continue to cook until chicken is done, about 30 minutes.

PER RECIPE: 1580 cal., 126 g. protein, 68 g. fat (13 sat., 28 poly.)
FOR 4 SERVINGS, 400 calories per serving

CHINESE CHICKEN WITH SNOW PEAS*

1 frying chicken (2½ pounds)
2 tablespoons cornstarch
2 slices fresh ginger or ¼ teaspoon powdered ginger

3 tablespoons oil
1 teaspoon salt
½ teaspoon monosodium glutamate
½ pound snow peas*, tips removed

If you have learned the special skill of the Chinese cooks, bone and dice the chicken. Or cut it into reasonably small pieces. Dredge the chicken in cornstarch. If you use powdered ginger, mix it with the cornstarch.

* See note on snow peas in section VII of the chapter on VEGETABLES.

Heat a large skillet; add the oil. Cut the ginger into tiny bits and add it. Fry the chicken in the oil until it is done, 8 to 10 minutes. Season with salt and monosodium glutamate. Add the snow peas and cook for 2 to 3 minutes more. Serve at once.

PER RECIPE: 1170 cal., 108 g. protein, 70 g. fat (12 sat., 27 poly.) FOR 4 SERVINGS, 290 calories per serving

CHINESE CHICKEN WITH BEAN SPROUTS

1 pound cooked chicken, cut into thin slices
4 tablespoons vegetable oil
2 teaspoons salt
Dash of pepper
½ cup chopped onion
¼ clove garlic, minced
¼ pound fresh mushrooms, sliced

1 green pepper, sliced
2 cups bean sprouts
1 cup chicken stock or stock substitute
1 teaspoon powdered ginger
2 tablespoons cornstarch
2 tablespoons soy sauce

Cook chicken in oil in a heavy skillet for a few minutes, stirring constantly. Season with salt and pepper. Add onion and garlic. Cook for 1 to 2 minutes, then add mushrooms, green pepper, bean sprouts, and chicken stock. Cover pan and simmer for 10 minutes.

Combine ginger, cornstarch, and soy sauce with ¼ cup water and add to skillet, continuing to cook and stir until juice thickens. Serve immediately with hot boiled rice.

PER RECIPE: 1560 cal., 110 g. protein, 110 g. fat (24 sat., 38 poly.) FOR 4 SERVINGS, 390 calories per serving

GREEN BEANS WITH CHICKEN GIBLETS

1 pound chicken giblets
1 small onion, minced
2 tablespoons oil
2 tablespoons flour

½ teaspoon thyme
Salt and pepper to taste
1 pound fresh green beans

Simmer giblets in salted water until tender, about ½ hour. The liver will cook more quickly than the heart or gizzard and can be removed and set aside after 10 minutes. Drain and chop giblets, reserving liquor. Fry onion in oil 5 minutes, add giblets, fry 2 minutes longer; then add flour, thyme, salt, and pepper, and mix well. Add ½ cup giblet broth and stir and cook until boiling. Keep hot.

Cook beans in a minimum of salted water until tender, about 15 minutes. Drain, place in heated serving dish, and pour giblet mixture over them.

PER RECIPE: 1180 cal., 105 g. protein, 46 g. fat (7 sat., 14 poly.)
FOR 6 SERVINGS, 200 calories per serving

BAKED CHICKEN SALAD WITH PEANUTS

1 frying chicken (2½ pounds), cut into quarters
1 teaspoon salt
¼ cup mayonnaise
2 tablespoons lemon juice
1 cup stock in which chicken was cooked thickened with
2 tablespoons flour
2 cups thinly sliced celery
¼ cup chopped onion
½ cup salted Spanish peanuts
1 cup crushed potato chips

Season chicken with salt and simmer in a covered pan with ½ inch of water in the bottom of the pan until the breast is fork-tender, for about ½ hour. Cut into bite-sized pieces, discarding bones and skin. Combine mayonnaise and lemon juice with thickened stock, add chicken, celery, onion, and peanuts to it, mix well, turn into oven-proof dish, sprinkle crushed potato chips over the top, and bake 20 minutes in a 350° oven. Serve hot or cold.

PER RECIPE: 2030 cal., 170 g. protein, 125 g. fat (30 sat., 45 poly.)
FOR 6 SERVINGS, 340 calories per serving

IV. BEANS AND PORK

PORK CHOPS WITH CHILI BEANS

4 boneless pork chops   1 cup canned tomatoes
(1 pound)   Salt to taste
1 (15¾-oz.) can chili
hot beans in chili
gravy

Brown pork chops on both sides in hot skillet; add contents
of can of chili beans, tomatoes, and salt. Reduce heat to simmer,
cover, and cook until pork chops are tender, about ½ hour.

Other less highly seasoned canned beans can be substituted,
and the dish can be prepared by putting the beans in the bottom
of the casserole, the chops on top. The tomato can be omitted,
or if used, poured over the chops. Cover the casserole and
bake for 1 hour at 350°. Check occasionally to be sure there is
enough moisture—add water or more tomato if needed.

PER RECIPE: 1180 cal., 116 g. protein, 43 g. fat (16 sat., 5 poly.)
FOR 4 SERVINGS, 300 calories per serving

BRAZILIAN BLACK BEANS (FEIJOADA)

This traditional dish of Brazil suggests the cassoulet of southern
France, and, like cassoulet, it has many versions. The black
beans, garlic, smoked meats, and onion are essential, but the
kinds and amounts of smoked meats can be varied. We suspect
that sun-dried meat was used in a dish of this kind.

½ pound smoked beef   1 large onion, minced
tongue   3 cloves garlic, minced
1 pound smoked lean   ½ cup chopped parsley
ham hocks   2 tablespoons oil
1 pound pork sausage   Salt to taste
2 pounds black beans

Parboil the smoked meats. Fry sausage for 10 minutes, drain
on absorbent paper, discarding drippings. Soak and simmer

beans as described in the introduction to the chapter on SOUPS. When beans have cooked for 2 hours add the meats and continue cooking for 2 hours more, adding water if necessary. Fry onion, garlic, and parsley lightly in oil, then add to beans with sausage. Add more salt, if desired.

Serve with hot boiled rice and a plate of peeled, sliced oranges.

PER RECIPE: 5710 cal., 326 g. protein, 339 g. fat (79 sat., 38 poly.)

FOR 12 SERVINGS, 480 calories per serving

BEAN AND BACON "CUTLETS"

1 cup chopped ripe
olives
2½ cups thick navy
bean purée
8 cups soft bread
crumbs
2 eggs

⅓ cup milk
Oil for deep fat frying
8 strips fried or broiled
bacon
8 thick sautéed,
unpeeled apple rings

Combine chopped ripe olives with bean purée and 1½ cups of the bread crumbs, blend thoroughly, and form into 8 "cutlets." Roll in remaining bread crumbs, patting them on; dip into thoroughly blended beaten eggs and milk, again into crumbs to form a thick coating. Fry in deep fat until golden brown. Lay a strip of bacon on each cutlet and serve with apple rings.

PER RECIPE: 2700 cal., 107 g. protein, 89 g. fat (21 sat., 9 poly.)

FOR 8 SERVINGS, 340 calories per serving

LENTILS AND SAUSAGE

2 cups lentils
2 onions, sliced
1 pound bulk pork
sausage

Salt and pepper to taste
Bouquet garni* if
desired

* Herbs such as thyme, bay leaf, and parsley tied together in a small piece of cheesecloth.

Soak lentils; then simmer until tender with onions, salt and pepper, and a bouquet garni if desired. The whole process requires about 3 hours.

Form patties of the sausage and fry in a skillet until partly done, for about 10 minutes. Drain on absorbent paper.

Drain the lentils, reserving the liquor. Remove the bouquet garni, if used. Place the lentils in the bottom of a shallow casserole, pour over them enough of the cooking liquid to just cover the lentils. Arrange the sausage patties on top and bake in a 350° oven until thoroughly hot, from 15 to 20 minutes.

PER RECIPE: 3160 cal., 155 g. protein, 154 g. fat (55 sat., 16 poly.) FOR 8 SERVINGS, 440 calories per serving

QUICK KIDNEY BEAN CASSEROLE

1 onion, chopped
1 green pepper, seeded and chopped
2 tablespoons oil
2 (15½-oz.) cans red kidney beans
1 (10½-oz.) can black bean soup, diluted with ½ cup sherry or water

1 clove garlic, minced
⅛ teaspoon ground cumin seeds (optional)
⅛ teaspoon dried tarragon (optional)
Salt and pepper to taste
¼ pound bulk sausage, cooked, drained, and broken into bits

Fry onion and green pepper in oil until onion is transparent, about 10 minutes. Drain kidney beans and rinse with cold water. Dilute black bean soup and combine all ingredients except sausage and place in a casserole. Top with cooked, crumbled sausage and heat in 350° oven until thoroughly hot, for 15 to 20 minutes.

PER RECIPE: 1600 cal., 69 g. protein, 67 g. fat (16 sat., 19 poly.) FOR 6 SERVINGS, 270 calories per serving

PORK AND BEANS WITH CAPERS

2 medium-sized onions, chopped
3 stalks celery, sliced
1 green pepper, diced
2 tablespoons oil
⅛ teaspoon marjoram
⅛ teaspoon thyme
Salt to taste

½ pound cooked pork (leftover roast, tenderloin, chops)
1 (1-pound) can Roman, great northern, or other beans
1 teaspoon capers
8 pimento-stuffed olives

Cook onion, celery, and green pepper in oil in a skillet until the onion is transparent. Add marjoram, thyme, and salt to taste. Cut cooked meat into bite-sized pieces; add it to the mixture in the skillet with the beans, capers, and olives and continue to cook only until thoroughly hot.

PER RECIPE: 1430 cal., 105 g. protein, 70 g. fat (18 sat., 20 poly.)
FOR 4 SERVINGS, 360 calories per serving

CHINESE PORK AND BEAN SPROUTS

¼ cup slivered almonds
2 tablespoons oil
2 teaspoons salt
1 pound lean pork, cut into thin slices
2 cups bean sprouts

1 cup chicken stock
2 cups sliced carrots
1 green pepper, cut into small pieces
2 tablespoons cornstarch
2 tablespoons soy sauce

Cook almonds in oil in a heavy skillet until golden brown; remove from pan and set aside. Add salt and pork. Cook over moderate heat until the meat is brown, from 5 to 10 minutes. Add bean sprouts, chicken stock, carrots, and green pepper. Cover pan and cook over low heat for 10 minutes. Blend together cornstarch, soy sauce, and ¼ cup water. Add to the ingredients in the skillet; cook and stir until juice thickens. Add almonds and serve immediately with hot boiled rice.

PER RECIPE: 1800 cal., 151 g. protein, 110 g. fat (27 sat., 24 poly.)
FOR 6 SERVINGS, 300 calories per serving

CHINESE PORK AND SNOW PEAS*

1 tablespoon oil
½ pound lean raw pork,
    cut into thin small
    slices
2 tablespoons soy sauce
1 cup fresh mushrooms,
    sliced

1 tablespoon oil
¼ pound snow peas*,
    tips removed
⅔ cup chicken stock or
    stock substitute
1 tablespoon cornstarch

Heat a heavy skillet, add 1 tablespoon oil and pork; cook and stir until well browned. Add soy sauce and set aside.

In a separate pan fry mushrooms in a second tablespoon of oil. Add them to the meat with snow peas and stock. Cover and cook over low heat for 3 minutes. Make a paste of cornstarch and ¼ cup water; add it to the meat mixture and cook and stir until thickened.

PER RECIPE: 870 cal., 82 g. protein, 56 g. fat (12 sat., 17 poly.)
FOR 4 SERVINGS, 220 calories per serving

V. BEANS AND LAMB

From Rome, from Paris, and from New Orleans come nearly alike versions of:

BEAN AND LAMB CASSEROLE

2 pounds navy beans
1 pound lamb shoulder,
    cut into cubes
2 tablespoons oil
1 large onion, chopped
2 tablespoons flour
1 tablespoon tomato
    purée
2 cloves garlic, minced
Salt and pepper to taste

A pinch of oregano and
    a bay leaf in the
    Italian version
A pinch of marjoram in
    the New Orleans dish
¼ pound small cooked
    mushrooms
½ cup chopped black
    olives and/or 2
    zucchini, sliced

* See note on snow peas in section VII of the chapter on VEGETABLES.

Soak and simmer beans as directed in the introduction to the chapter on SOUPS. Brown meat cubes in oil, add onion, and continue to cook for 2 to 3 minutes, then sprinkle meat with flour. Mix thoroughly. Add tomato purée, garlic, salt and pepper, and other seasonings if used, and warm water to cover. Cook gently for 2 hours. Drain beans and add to meat with mushrooms and olives or zucchini, simmer together for 5 minutes, or place in 350° oven until thoroughly hot.

PER RECIPE: 4130 cal., 291 g. protein, 76 g. fat (24 sat., 24 poly.) FOR 10 SERVINGS, 410 calories per serving

VI. BEANS WITH FISH OR SEAFOOD

BEANS AND CLAMS

½ pound dried navy beans
1 (7½-oz.) can minced clams
1 sliver garlic
6 green onions with tops, sliced

Salt to taste
1 pound fresh green beans, cut into 1-inch pieces
1 tablespoon chopped parsley
1 lemon

Soak and simmer beans as directed in the introduction to the chapter on SOUPS, continuing to cook until beans are tender. Drain, reserving liquor. Combine in a casserole with drained clams, garlic, onion, and ½ cup of bean liquor; add salt, and place in slow (250–300°) oven while you cook the green beans in a minimum of salted water until just tender, 10 to 15 minutes. Drain green beans and add to casserole with parsley, mix well, and serve with quarters of lemon.

PER RECIPE: 1130 cal., 90 g. protein, 10 g. fat (1 sat., 3 poly.) FOR 4 SERVINGS, 280 calories per serving

BEAN SPROUTS AND SHRIMPS

1 pound fresh or frozen shrimps
4 tablespoons soy sauce
1 pound bean sprouts

Peel fresh shrimps and cook 5 minutes in boiling water to which soy sauce has been added. Cook frozen shrimps according to directions on package. When shrimps are done, remove and keep them hot while you cook the bean sprouts in the same water. Combine drained sprouts with shrimps, serve with hot boiled rice.

PER RECIPE: 660 cal., 123 g. protein, 7 g. fat (2 sat., 1 poly.) FOR 4 SERVINGS, 170 calories per serving

RED BEANS WITH SALT COD

1 pound salt cod fish
2 tablespoons flour
¼ cup oil plus 1
  tablespoon
1 pound red beans
3 onions, chopped
2 cloves garlic, minced

Celery tops, lettuce
  leaves, and other
  greens, chopped
Salt and pepper to taste
1 small hot red pepper
  or a few drops
  Tabasco sauce
2 tablespoons chopped
  parsley

Soak cod in cold water overnight. Dry, cut into individual portions, and remove bones. Roll in flour and fry in ¼ cup oil. Drain on absorbent paper. Keep hot.

Soak and simmer beans as described in the introduction to the chapter on SOUPS. Add 2 onions, 1 clove garlic, celery tops and other greens, salt and pepper, and continue to simmer until the beans are tender. Drain them, put them on a hot platter, and arrange the cod fish on top.

Meanwhile fry the remaining onion and garlic, the red pepper, if used, and the parsley in 1 tablespoon oil until well blended. Add Tabasco sauce if desired. Place a heaping teaspoon of this mixture on each piece of cod.

PER RECIPE: 3030 cal., 244 g. protein, 80 g. fat (7 sat., 39 poly.) FOR 8 SERVINGS, 350 calories per serving

VEGETABLES

The four preceding chapters have been made up of recipes for the main dish of the meal. The term "side dish" has gone out of fashion, but the intent was to describe an accompaniment to the meat, fish, poultry, or other *pièce de résistance*. The recipes in this chapter are for "side dishes" of this kind. We hope the cook who has limited her vegetable cookery to boiling, draining, and then seasoning with salt and a pat of butter will find recipes among the forty in this chapter that will bring variety and pleasure to her dinner table.

I. GREEN BEANS

Whether they are called string, pole, snap, or green beans, they are at their best when picked young, eaten as soon thereafter as possible, and cooked briefly in a minimum of boiling salted water to retain their flavor, color, and crispness. The nearest we have come in this country to the marvelous *fagiolini* of Italy or the delicate *haricots verts* of France has been to pick beans from our own garden while they are still quite immature. They are at their best when not much bigger than a kitchen match.

Frozen green beans can be used in an emergency; even when canned they have possibilities. But cooking time should be shortened accordingly. Time is the worst enemy of the string bean—too much time on the vine, too long at the grocer's, too much time in cooking. If long cooking is needed to make them tender, throw them out or at least resolve to make a better selection next time.

But Americans are fortunate in having good fresh green beans in our markets almost all year. We like them cooked as described in the previous paragraph, and seasoned only with salt or with lemon juice and olive oil. Or add a few slivers of toasted almonds or some sautéed mushrooms. Green beans lend themselves to many good combinations. Here are a baker's dozen for your enjoyment, with space in the margins for you to write in your own variations.

BAKED GREEN BEANS

1 pound fresh green beans
1 (10½-oz.) can cream of mushroom soup
¼ cup skim milk

1 (2-oz.) can sliced mushrooms
½ teaspoon salt or to taste

Cut beans into 2-inch lengths; cook briefly, about 5 minutes, in minimum amount of salted water until partially tender. Drain and transfer to casserole. Combine soup, milk, drained mushrooms, and salt; pour over beans and bake in 350° oven for 30 minutes.

PER RECIPE: 520 cal., 18 g. protein, 25 g. fat (9 sat., 2 poly.) FOR 4 SERVINGS, 130 calories per serving

This recipe for baked green beans is basic and is easily varied with good results. For example, omit the sliced mushrooms, season the soup with 1 teaspoon soy sauce, and top the casserole with French-fried onions (1 can, 3½ oz.).

PER RECIPE: 720 cal., 18 g. protein, 40 g. fat (8 sat., 11 poly.) FOR 6 SERVINGS, 120 calories per serving

Or top the casserole with ¼ cup grated Cheddar cheese, or less than that amount of Parmesan cheese.

PER RECIPE: 860 cal., 43 g. protein, 54 g. fat (22 sat., 10 poly.) FOR 4 SERVINGS, 220 calories per serving

GREEN BEANS SUPREME

2 slices bacon
1 tablespoon oil
¼ cup chopped onion
1 (10½-oz.) can cream
of celery soup

⅓ cup milk
1 pound fresh green
beans, or
2 (10-oz.) packages
frozen green beans

Cook bacon until crisp. Remove and crumble. Discard drippings and replace with oil. Cook onion in the oil for 5 minutes, blend in soup and milk. Meanwhile cook beans in a minimum amount of boiling salted water for about 10 minutes, until nearly tender. Drain and combine with the other ingredients and heat thoroughly. Serve with crumbled bacon on top.

PER RECIPE: 670 cal., 22 g. protein, 40 g. fat (7 sat., 17 poly.) FOR 4 SERVINGS, 170 calories per serving

GREEN BEAN CASSEROLE

This dish is prepared with an herb-seasoned white sauce instead of the canned soups of the two preceding recipes. Let your own taste dictate the herbs.

1 pound green beans
2 tablespoons oil
¼ cup flour
1 teaspoon salt
2 cups meat or
vegetable stock

¼ teaspoon basil or
marjoram
½ teaspoon dry
mustard
2 chopped pimentos
2 tablespoons grated
Parmesan cheese

Cut green beans into short lengths and cook in a minimum amount of boiling salted water until beans are nearly tender, 8 to 10 minutes. Drain and plunge them into cold water to preserve crispness and color.

Meanwhile prepare white sauce with oil, flour, salt, and stock. Stir into it the basil or marjoram, dry mustard, and pimento. Combine with beans in a casserole; top with grated cheese. Bake in 350° oven for 20 to 30 minutes.

PER RECIPE: 570 cal., 21 g. protein, 33 g. fat (2 sat., 15 poly.)
FOR 4 SERVINGS, 140 calories per serving

GREEN BEAN SUCCOTASH

Equally good indoors and out, this is an easy recipe to use for an outdoor barbecue.

1 onion, chopped
2 tablespoons oil
¼ cup catsup
1 teaspoon
  Worcestershire sauce
1 package frozen whole
  kernel corn, or

1 (12-oz.) can whole
  kernel corn
1 pound fresh green
  beans, or
2 packages frozen cut
  green beans
Tabasco sauce or red
  pepper to taste

Cook onion in oil until golden; add catsup and Worcestershire sauce. Add frozen corn to this with 2 or 3 tablespoons of water and cook until corn is thawed. If canned corn is used, simply add to mixture.

Cook beans in a small amount of boiling salted water until just tender, about 15 minutes. If they are prepared in advance, chill them in cold water at this stage.

A few minutes before serving, add drained beans to onion-corn mixture, heat thoroughly, adding Tabasco sauce or red pepper if "hot" beans are desired.

PER RECIPE: 640 cal., 14 g. protein, 30 g. fat (3 sat., 15 poly.)
FOR 6 SERVINGS, 105 calories per serving

FRIED GREEN BEANS I

We cook these by two different methods, the first developed especially for our outdoor grill.

1 pound fresh green beans
1 slice bacon

To prepare beans ahead of time for last-minute frying, cook them whole, in a minimum of salted water until nearly tender, 8 to 10 minutes. Meanwhile cut bacon into small bits and cook in a large skillet until nearly crisp. Drain beans, plunge into cold water for a few minutes. Drain again and add to the bacon. They are now ready to finish cooking on the outdoor grill when the rest of the meal is nearly ready. Cook and stir over fairly high heat until lightly browned.

If the beans are cooked just before serving, they can be put directly into the skillet without chilling.

PER RECIPE: 520 cal., 18 g. protein, 25 g. fat (9 sat., 2 poly.)
FOR 4 SERVINGS, 130 calories per serving

FRIED GREEN BEANS II

1 pound green beans
2 tablespoons oil
Salt and pepper to taste

A few flakes of chopped dehydrated onion (optional)
1 teaspoon lemon juice (optional)

Put the whole beans in a skillet with the oil, salt and pepper, onion flakes if desired, and ½ cup water. Cover tightly and cook over low heat until the beans are tender, about 15 minutes. Remove the cover and continue cooking until water has evaporated and beans are slightly browned, stirring occasionally. Add lemon juice, if desired, before serving.

PER RECIPE: 380 cal., 8 g. protein, 29 g. fat (2 sat., 15 poly.)
FOR 4 SERVINGS, 100 calories per serving

GREEN BEANS IN TOMATO SAUCE

1 clove garlic	1 pound green beans,
2 tablespoons oil	tips removed
½ cup tomato sauce	½ teaspoon salt
	1 teaspoon paprika

Heat the garlic in the oil for 1 or 2 minutes; discard the garlic before it turns brown. Add the tomato sauce, beans, salt, and paprika; cover and cook over low heat until beans are tender, 15 to 20 minutes.

PER RECIPE: 420 cal., 10 g. protein, 29 g. fat (2 sat., 14 poly.)
FOR 4 SERVINGS, 110 calories per serving

GREEN BEANS WITH YOGURT AND SAVORY

1 pound green beans	4 ounces yogurt
½ teaspoon salt or to	¼ teaspoon savory
taste	

Cook beans in minimum amount of salted water until tender, 15 to 20 minutes. Drain off water, stir in yogurt and savory, and return to heat until thoroughly hot.

The yogurt will have a curdled appearance. If you wish to avoid this, prepare ½ cup thin white sauce, add yogurt and savory to it and pour over the beans.

PER RECIPE: 400 cal., 21 g. protein, 16 g. fat (8 sat., trace poly.)
FOR 4 SERVINGS, 100 calories per serving

GREEN BEANS SOUTHERN STYLE

1 ounce salt pork, cubed	1 teaspoon salt
2 pounds green beans	1 teaspoon sugar

Cook the salt pork in a small quantity of water until almost tender. Break beans and add them to the kettle with salt and sugar. Allow to boil at high heat for 10 minutes, then reduce heat and continue cooking until all the liquid has disappeared, stirring occasionally.

PER RECIPE: 470 cal., 17 g. protein, 23 g. fat (9 sat., 3 poly.) FOR 8 SERVINGS, 60 calories per serving

MIXED VEGETABLES

1 cup green beans, cut into 1-inch pieces
1 small onion, sliced
½ cup sliced cabbage

2 tablespoons brown sugar
2 bay leaves
Salt to taste
½ cup blanched peanuts

Put all ingredients except peanuts in a pan with a minimum amount of water. Bring to a boil and simmer 20 minutes. Add peanuts and serve with a hot relish.

PER RECIPE: 580 cal., 43 g. protein, 64 g. fat (14 sat., 18 poly.) FOR 4 SERVINGS, 150 calories per serving

STRING BEANS

This recipe is from Korea.

½ pound chopped lean beef
1 green onion, chopped
1 teaspoon oil
2 tablespoons soy sauce

1 tablespoon sesame seeds
1 teaspoon sugar
1 pound green beans

Mix together all ingredients except the beans; cook and stir until the meat is done.

Meanwhile cook the beans 5 minutes in a small amount of salted water. Drain the beans and add them to the beef mixture. Cover and cook over low heat about 10 minutes until the beans are just tender but still crisp.

PER RECIPE: 400 cal., 34 g. protein, 15 g. fat (4 sat., 5 poly.) FOR 4 SERVINGS, 100 calories per serving

DUTCH OVEN GREEN BEANS

2 tablespoons oil
1 medium-sized onion,
  sliced
2 stalks celery, sliced
1 green pepper, chopped

1 pound green beans
1 clove garlic, minced
½ teaspoon salt
1 teaspoon basil

Put the oil and all the vegetables except the beans in a Dutch oven or other heavy pot with tight-fitting lid and cook over medium heat for 5 minutes, stirring occasionally. Add the beans and garlic and ½ cup water, season with salt and basil, cover the kettle, and reduce the heat. Simmer until beans are done, about 15 minutes.

PER RECIPE: 460 cal., 11 g. protein, 29 g. fat (2 sat., 14 poly.)
FOR 4 SERVINGS, 120 calories per serving

BEANS AND BEAN SPROUTS

2 pounds fresh green
  beans, cut diagonally,
  or
3 (10-oz.) packages
  French-cut frozen green
  beans

2 (1-pound) cans bean
  sprouts
2 (10½-oz.) cans cream
  of mushroom soup
1 (3½-oz.) can
  French-fried onions

Cook the beans in a minimum amount of salted water until nearly tender, about 10 minutes. Drain the bean sprouts and rinse in cold water. Arrange beans and bean sprouts in layers and spread undiluted mushroom soup over each layer, ending with the soup. Bake for 20 minutes at 350°, crumble French-fried onions and sprinkle over top, return to oven for an additional 10 minutes.

PER RECIPE: 1330 cal., 55 g. protein, 42 g. fat (6 sat., 19 poly.)
FOR 12 SERVINGS, 110 calories per serving

BEANS BORDELAISE

½ pound green beans	1 green onion with top
½ pound fresh or	2 tablespoons oil
frozen lima beans	2 tablespoons dry red
1 clove garlic	wine
2 anchovies	

Cook green beans 10 minutes and lima beans 20 minutes separately until each is nearly done, then combine and finish cooking together. Drain. Mince garlic, anchovies, and green onion and fry 2 minutes in oil. Add beans and wine, cook and stir until thoroughly hot.

PER RECIPE: 650 cal., 23 g. protein, 30 g. fat (2 sat., 16 poly.) FOR 4 SERVINGS, 160 calories per serving

II. WAX BEANS

We are so fond of green beans that we tend to forget their yellowish cousin, the wax bean. There are also varieties with piebald markings and old wax beans which tend to have a brownish tinge. Presumably wax beans could be used in some of the foregoing recipes but they would contribute less flavor. Wax beans are so bland that they are best in recipes in which other flavors take over. Wax beans are also available fresh most of the year, but it is not always easy to get them young enough to be at their best. For ordinary cooking the same rule holds as for green beans: brief cooking and a small quantity of water. A few grains of nutmeg will enhance the flavor, or try:

WAX BEANS PAPRIKA

1 pound fresh wax beans	1 tablespoon paprika
1 tablespoon oil	1 tablespoon capers
1 teaspoon salt	

Combine beans, oil, salt, and enough water to cover the bottom of the pan, and cook, covered, until the beans are tender, about 15 minutes. Remove cover, season with paprika and capers, and simmer uncovered until the water has evaporated.

PER RECIPE: 270 cal., 10 g. protein, 15 g. fat (2 sat., 8 poly.)
FOR 4 SERVINGS, 70 calories per serving

FRIED WAX BEANS AND GREEN PEPPERS

1 *pound fresh wax beans*   2 *green peppers, cut into*
2 *tablespoons oil*   *strips*
                                                      Salt to taste

Cook beans in minimum amount of salted water until nearly tender, about 10 minutes. Drain beans and fry in oil with pepper strips until lightly browned, stirring occasionally.

PER RECIPE: 390 cal., 8 g. protein, 29 g. fat (2 sat., 14 poly.)
FOR 4 SERVINGS, 100 calories per serving

PIQUANT WAX BEANS

1 *pound wax beans*   1 *tablespoon tarragon*
2 *slices bacon, diced*   *vinegar*
¼ *cup minced onion*   ⅛ *teaspoon freshly*
1 *teaspoon sugar*   *ground pepper*

Cook beans in minimum amount of salted water until tender, about 15 minutes. Fry bacon. Remove from pan and add onion; cook until golden brown. Drain both bacon and onion on absorbent paper. Crumble bacon.

Drain beans. Add sugar, vinegar, and pepper and heat thoroughly. Serve with bacon and onion sprinkled on top.

PER RECIPE: 260 cal., 12 g. protein, 10 g. fat (3 sat., 2 poly.)
FOR 4 SERVINGS, 70 calories per serving

III. RELUCTANTLY, BROAD BEANS

The broad bean, *Vicia faba*, vaguely suggests a misshapen green bean that is five times too big. The plant is big, too; it must have been a giant broad-bean vine that Jack of Jack-and-the-Beanstalk climbed. Living in England, we were introduced to the broad bean and had the impression that they are still eaten there by Britons who like to cling to the old ways—when no better beans were available. The Englishman who is keen about Morris dancing and church bell-ringing groups, who drinks sherry but never cocktails, is apt to speak kindly of broad beans. British vegetable cookery being what it is, we were not surprised that when they served broad beans to us our appreciation was decidedly limited. But when we took some home to cook ourselves, the result was not much better.

In Italy there is a *fava* season in the spring and people out walking are apt to pick them growing wild and eat a few of them raw. Our experimentation with this in Sardinia led us to conclude that it is an interesting, quaint custom. Still, broad beans are edible and the old Romans ate them for the good reason that no "real" beans (*Phaseolus* species) were available. We probably give the broad bean less than its due. Try one of these recipes:

BROAD BEANS WITH HAM

¼ pound lean ham, diced	2 pounds broad beans, shelled
2 tablespoons oil	1 cup tomato juice
1 clove garlic	⅛ teaspoon dried basil
1 small onion, minced	Salt and pepper to taste

Fry ham in oil with garlic and onion for 5 minutes; remove garlic. Combine with beans and tomato juice in kettle with tightly fitting cover; season with basil, salt, and pepper. Cover and simmer for 1½ hours or more, until beans are very tender. Add more tomato juice if beans become too dry.

PER RECIPE: 800 cal., 55 g. protein, 34 g. fat (3 sat., 15 poly.) FOR 8 SERVINGS, 100 calories per serving

BROAD BEANS WITH BASIL

1 onion, sliced
2 tablespoons olive oil
2 pounds broad beans, shelled

3 stalks celery, thinly sliced
1 clove garlic (optional)
1 teaspoon basil
Salt and pepper to taste

Fry the onion in oil, add the beans, and cook for 2 to 3 minutes, then add the rest of the ingredients with enough water to cover the bottom of the pan. Cover pan tightly and simmer for 20 minutes or until beans are tender.

PER RECIPE: 650 cal., 29 g. protein, 30 g. fat (3 sat., 3 poly.) FOR 8 SERVINGS, 80 calories per serving

IV. BEANS COMBINED WITH OTHER VEGETABLES

SPANISH CABBAGE

½ pound dried chick-peas or 1 (15-oz.) can
1 medium-sized cabbage, chopped
3 tablespoons oil
1 teaspoon minced onion
1 clove garlic

¼ pound ham, minced
2 cups chopped tomatoes
Salt and pepper to taste
2 red pimentos, cut into strips

If dried chick-peas are used, soak and simmer as described for beans in the introduction to the chapter on soups. To re-

move the loosened skins, drain the peas and rub them between two towels.

In another pan boil the cabbage, uncovered, for 10 minutes.
In a large skillet fry onion and garlic in oil. When soft, add
ham and tomatoes. Cook 5 minutes; season well with salt and
pepper. Add the drained, cooked or canned chick-peas and
cabbage; cook all together until thoroughly hot. Garnish with
pimento.

PER RECIPE: 1710 cal., 88 g. protein, 65 g. fat (9 sat., 29 poly.)
FOR 8 SERVINGS, 210 calories per serving

BRAISED CELERY AND LIMA BEANS

1 (10-oz.) package frozen lima beans	2 tablespoons oil
5 large stalks celery	1 teaspoon beef-stock base or Ac'cent

Cook lima beans as directed on package, being careful not
to overcook them. Meanwhile slice celery and cook it over
medium heat in oil in a skillet with a cover until transparent.
Season with beef-stock base or Ac'cent, add drained, cooked
lima beans, and heat thoroughly.

PER RECIPE: 560 cal., 19 g. protein, 30 g. fat (2 sat., 15 poly.)
FOR 4 SERVINGS, 140 calories per serving

TUTÚ OF BLACK BEANS

This is a dish of black beans from Brazil, where it is traditionally
served with meat—pork chops, spareribs, or beefsteak.

2 cups cooked or canned black beans	1 bay leaf
4 tablespoons flour	1 onion, sliced
Salt and pepper to taste	2 tomatoes, peeled
	2 tablespoons oil

Purée the beans in a blender or food mill. Add the flour mixed
to a paste in a little water, salt and pepper, and bay leaf and

cook and stir over medium heat until thick—the consistency of porridge. Discard bay leaf. Spread in a wide deep dish and cover with the following topping:

Cook onion and tomatoes in oil, add salt. When onion and tomatoes are tender, spread on top of bean mixture. Heat in oven only until thoroughly hot.

PER RECIPE: 930 cal., 37 g. protein, 31 g. fat (2 sat., 15 poly.) FOR 6 SERVINGS, 150 calories per serving

BEANS AND SAUERKRAUT

2 tablespoons oil	2 cups sauerkraut,
2 medium onions, sliced	drained
1 (15-oz.) can great	½ teaspoon poppy seeds
northern beans	(optional)

Pour oil in the bottom of a casserole; next put in a layer of sliced onion, then the beans with their liquor, then the sauerkraut on top, sprinkled with poppy seeds if desired. Bake in a slow (250°) oven, covered, for 1 hour.

PER RECIPE: 820 cal., 34 g. protein, 31 g. fat (2 sat., 15 poly.) FOR 4 SERVINGS, 210 calories per serving

LIMA BEANS AND APPLES

A good accompaniment for ham, smoked beef tongue, or curried meat.

2 cups (1 pound)	4 tart apples, sliced but
dried lima beans	not peeled
2 large onions, chopped	½ teaspoon allspice
3 tablespoons oil	¼ teaspoon turmeric
	Salt and pepper to taste

Soak and simmer lima beans as described in the introduction to the chapter on SOUPS. Drain, reserving liquor. Fry onion in oil in a large skillet. When golden, add apple and seasonings.

Cook slowly, and stir, for a few minutes, then add cooked lima beans and ½ cup bean liquor. Cover and simmer for 10 minutes, adding more liquor if necessary.

PER RECIPE: 2410 cal., 100 g. protein, 52 g. fat (5 sat., 25 poly.) FOR 8 SERVINGS, 300 calories per serving

BEANS AND BANANAS

If you enjoy fried bananas accompanying a curry, as we do, you will like these banana patties. We have eaten a similar dish in Mexico, made with the big *plátanos*—cooking bananas.

3 bananas	*1 cup cooked navy*
3 tablespoons flour	*beans, drained*
Salt to taste	*2 tablespoons oil*
1 tablespoon lemon juice	

Mash bananas, add flour, salt, and lemon juice and blend together. Combine with beans, shape into patties, and brown on both sides in oil in a heavy skillet over moderate heat.

PER RECIPE: 820 cal., 20 g. protein, 30 g. fat (2 sat., 15 poly.) FOR 4 SERVINGS, 210 calories per serving

SUCCOTASH

Succotash dates back at least to early days in New England where it apparently received its name from the local Indian name *sauquaquatash*. How this bean had found its way to New England from Peru, where it had been grown for centuries, is not quite clear, but the origin must have been known even then as the bean was called by the name of Peru's largest city, Lima. The ancient Peruvians also grew corn, and perhaps they had their own version of succotash.

1 cup cooked fresh or
frozen whole kernel
corn*
1 cup cooked fresh or
frozen lima beans*

2 tablespoons oil
Salt and freshly ground
pepper to taste
2 ounces slivered
pimento (optional)

Combine and heat together corn and lima beans in the oil.
Season with salt and pepper, and pimento if desired.

PER RECIPE: 670 cal., 19 g. protein, 31 g. fat (2 sat., 15 poly.)
FOR 4 SERVINGS, 170 calories per serving

GLORIFIED SUCCOTASH

4 tablespoons flour
2 tablespoons oil
1 teaspoon salt
¼ teaspoon pepper
1½ cups skim milk
¼ cup grated cheese,
Parmesan or American
¼ cup pimento, in small
pieces

1 package frozen baby
lima beans
1 package frozen whole
kernel corn
½ cup green onion tops,
in ½-inch pieces
1 cup bread crumbs
mixed with 2
tablespoons oil

Make a white sauce by stirring the flour into the oil, adding
salt, pepper, and milk. Cook and stir until thick. Add cheese
and pimento.

Cook lima beans and corn according to directions on the
packages. Combine with white sauce, add onion tops, transfer
to oiled baking dish. Top with oiled crumbs and bake in 350°
oven for about ½ hour.

PER RECIPE: 1730 cal., 62 g. protein, 71 g. fat (9 sat., 30 poly.)
FOR 6 SERVINGS, 290 calories per serving

* Packaged frozen succotash is also available.

V. ADDITIONS TO ANY MEAL

HUNGARIAN PEASE PUDDING

This dish is often served as an accompaniment to smoked meat.

1 pound split peas	1 teaspoon paprika
1 medium-sized onion,	1 teaspoon chili powder
chopped	1 bouillon cube
2 tablespoons oil	Salt to taste
2 tablespoons flour	Dash Tabasco sauce

Soak and simmer peas as directed for beans in the introduction to the chapter on soups, adding onion before simmering. Total soak-and-simmer time is about 3 hours, or, if peas are soaked overnight, 1 hour of cooking is usually sufficient.

Heat oil in frying pan, add flour, paprika, and chili powder and cook until browned. Dissolve bouillon cube in 1 cup of hot water, add this to the frying pan, and bring to a boil, stirring constantly. Add peas, season with salt and Tabasco sauce if desired. Continue to cook and stir until thoroughly heated.

PER RECIPE: 1940 cal., 113 g. protein, 33 g. fat (3 sat., 17 poly.) FOR 10 SERVINGS, 190 calories per serving

FRIJOLES REFRITOS

The translation of the name of this dish, known as the national dish of Mexico (nacionales), is refried beans. They are prepared by mashing cooked (baked or boiled) beans as they fry in a skillet. In Mexico they are served in many ways, but usually as a separate course just before dessert, generally accompanied by a grated white cheese which we do not have in the United States. The nearest equivalent we have discovered is dry-curd cottage cheese forced through a strainer.

The cooked beans ordinarily used in Mexico to prepare the

refritos are called *frijoles de olla.* You will find the recipe in the chapter on BEAN POTS. The *olla* refers to the clay pot in which the beans are cooked, often over charcoal.

2 tablespoons oil
6 cups cooked beans,
  frijoles de olla, or other
  baked or canned beans

½ cup dry-curd cottage
  cheese

Heat oil in heavy skillet; add beans. Fry until beans form a mass which leaves the sides of the pan, mashing and stirring with a wooden spoon continuously. Form into rolls about the size and shape of a small sweet potato. Force cottage cheese through potato ricer or sieve and sprinkle on top of each serving.

PER RECIPE: 2500 cal., 114 g. protein, 121 g. fat (36 sat., 25 poly.)

FOR 10 SERVINGS, 250 calories per serving

OLD-FASHIONED PEASE PUDDING

Pease porridge hot
Pease porridge cold
Pease porridge in the pot
Nine days old.

Some like it hot
Some like it cold
Some like it in the pot
Nine days old.

Most of us know the nursery rhyme and the clapping game we played as children when we recited it, but most of us probably have never eaten it either hot, cold, or nine days old. Pease porridge, or pease pudding, has a smooth texture and a delicate flavor, and can be included in almost any meal, especially where it gives contrast with highly seasoned foods.

4 cups split peas
1 tablespoon oil

Salt and pepper to taste
3 eggs

Soak and simmer peas as described for beans in the introduction to the chapter on SOUPS, but note that split peas cook in less time than beans. Drain and put through a food mill or colander. Add oil, salt and pepper, and unbeaten eggs, blending thoroughly. Oil a pudding mold or small mixing bowl, put the mixture in it. Cover the mold or bowl with waxed paper tightly secured with string. Steam the pudding 1 hour. Turn it out on heated plate and slice at the table.

PER RECIPE: 3110 cal., 214 g. protein, 39 g. fat (9 sat., 13 poly.) FOR 10 SERVINGS, 310 calories per serving

VI. GREEN PEAS

Green peas are at their best when they have not developed to full maturity, are freshly picked and shelled just before cooking. Unfortunately the season for fresh green peas, a cool-weather crop, is very short, and we must make-do with frozen or canned peas. Here are some cooking suggestions for both fresh and frozen peas.

GREEN PEAS ITALIAN STYLE

¼ pound Canadian
bacon or Italian
prosciutto
2 onions, chopped

2 tablespoons oil
2 pounds fresh peas, or
2 packages frozen peas
Salt and pepper to taste

Cut Canadian bacon or *prosciutto* into small pieces and cook with onion in oil for 5 minutes. Add ½ cup water, peas, and salt and pepper. Cover pan and cook over low heat until peas are done, 10 to 15 minutes.

PER RECIPE: 900 cal., 48 g. protein, 46 g. fat (8 sat., 16 poly.) FOR 6 SERVINGS, 150 calories per serving

GREEN PEAS AND FRANKFURTERS

2 pounds fresh peas
Salt to taste
2 skinless frankfurters,
sliced

2 tablespoons oil
½ onion, chopped
(optional)

Shell peas and cook in minimum amount of slightly salted water until tender, from 5 to 20 minutes, depending on maturity of the peas.

Brown frankfurter slices in oil. If onion is used, cook it with the frankfurter. When peas are done, drain and add to the frankfurter, serve at once.

PER RECIPE: 880 cal., 35 g. protein, 58 g. fat (14 sat., 16 poly.) FOR 4 SERVINGS, 220 calories per serving

GREEN PEA RING

2 tablespoons oil	1 cup puréed green peas
2 tablespoons flour	Salt and pepper to taste
½ cup skim milk	3 eggs, separated

Make a white sauce of the oil, flour, and milk. Add puréed peas, and salt and pepper. Beat the egg yolks well and combine with the pea mixture, then carefully fold in the stiffly beaten whites. Pour into an oiled ring mold and place the mold in a pan of hot water. Bake in a moderate oven, 350°, until firm, about ½ hour.

PER RECIPE: 720 cal., 31 g. protein, 46 g. fat (9 sat., 16 poly.) FOR 4 SERVINGS, 180 calories per serving

PEAS AND SQUASH CASSEROLE

1 medium-sized onion, chopped	½ pound yellow summer squash, or
2 tablespoons oil	½ pound zucchini, cut into ½-inch slices
¼ cup flour	
Salt and pepper to taste	3 packages frozen peas or 2 (1-pound) cans
1 cup skim milk	
¼ cup grated Cheddar cheese	½ cup coarse cracker crumbs

Cook onion in oil until transparent. Stir in flour, salt and pepper; add milk and cook and stir until thickened. Stir in cheese, then add squash, thawed, frozen (or drained, canned) peas, and crumbs. Put in oiled casserole and bake at 350° for 45 minutes.

PER RECIPE: 1430 cal., 71 g. protein, 46 g. fat (8 sat., 17 poly.) FOR 8 SERVINGS, 180 calories per serving

GREEN PEAS FRENCH STYLE

2 pounds fresh peas
2 tablespoons oil
8 or 10 green onions or
  shallots, cut into
  ½-inch pieces

¼ teaspoon salt
3 or 4 lettuce leaves

Shell peas. Put oil in a pan with a tight cover. Add peas, onion or shallots, and salt. Wash lettuce leaves and place, dripping wet, over peas. Cover tightly and cook over low heat, taking care not to overcook. The cooking time varies from 5 to 20 minutes depending on the age of the peas. Discard lettuce.

PER RECIPE: 590 cal., 23 g. protein, 31 g. fat (2 sat., 14 poly.) FOR 4 SERVINGS, 150 calories per serving

CAULIFLOWER WITH PEAS

1 head cauliflower
2 teaspoons salt
3 tablespoons flour
2 tablespoons oil
2 cups skim milk

1 pound fresh peas, or
1 package frozen peas
Dash of nutmeg
  (optional)

Remove all outside leaves from the head of cauliflower. With a sharp, pointed knife, cut away as much of the stem as possible but leave the head whole, hollow out the stem to the depth of an inch or more. Place the cauliflower, stem end down, in a deep kettle, add 1 teaspoon salt and ½ cup boiling water. Cover kettle and cook over low heat until the cauliflower is fork-tender, about 20 minutes.

Meanwhile prepare the white sauce with the flour, oil, milk, and 1 teaspoon salt. Shell peas and cook in a minimum of salted water until just tender; drain and add to the white sauce. Place cauliflower in a heated serving dish; pour white sauce and peas over it and sprinkle lightly with nutmeg, if desired.

PER RECIPE: 750 cal., 40 g. protein, 30 g. fat (2 sat., 14 poly.) FOR 6 SERVINGS, 130 calories per serving

VII. SNOW PEAS

Chinese peas are also called Chinese pea pods, sugar peas, and snow peas. The Chinese use these sparingly because they are difficult to grow and therefore expensive, but even in small quantities their delicate flavor, delightful crispness, and fresh green color add much to many recipes. They can be added to any Chinese meat and vegetable dish.

Snow peas are now sometimes available in the regular supermarkets as well as in Chinese food shops. We change our menu, if necessary, to include them whenever they appear. They are tender pods in which the peas are just beginning to form, and they are eaten pod and all. They can be eaten as a separate vegetable as well as added to other dishes.

SNOW PEAS

½ pound snow peas
1 tablespoon oil
Salt to taste

1 teaspoon soy sauce, or
monosodium glutamate

Remove the tops and tails from the pea pods and wash thoroughly. Heat a skillet, add the oil, then the snow peas with whatever water clings to them from the washing. Cook for 1 minute, stirring constantly. Then add salt, soy sauce or monosodium glutamate, and 1 tablespoon of water. Cover the pan, reduce the heat, and simmer gently for 2 or 3 minutes. They should not be cooked long enough to lose their crispness. Serve immediately.

PER RECIPE: 200 cal., 5 g. protein, 15 g. fat (1 sat., 7 poly.) FOR 4 SERVINGS, 50 calories per serving

VIII. BEAN SPROUTS

Bean sprouts served as a vegetable add the crispness so often lacking in our meals. They are best with soy sauce, onion, garlic, pepper, or other flavorful seasonings.

BEAN SPROUTS AS A VEGETABLE

1 stalk celery, sliced thinly
1 small onion, sliced
½ green pepper, cut into strips
2 tablespoons oil

1 clove garlic (optional)
1 (1-pound) can bean sprouts
1 tablespoon soy sauce
Salt and pepper to taste

Cook celery, onion, and green pepper in oil for about 3 minutes. (A clove of garlic can be added for flavor, then removed). Add bean sprouts and soy sauce. Cover and cook gently for about 8 minutes. Add salt, if necessary, and pepper.

Or omit the celery, garlic, and green pepper and season instead with shallots in place of the onion, and add a speck of red pepper and 2 tablespoons prepared sesame seeds (see directions in the Rice and Bean Sprouts recipe in the chapter on LUNCH OR SUPPER).

PER RECIPE: 590 cal., 20 g. protein, 46 g. fat (3 sat., 17 poly.) FOR 8 SERVINGS, 70 calories per serving

IX. PEANUTS

CREAMED CELERY WITH PEANUTS

8 outside stalks celery,   1 cup white sauce
   cut into 3-inch lengths   Salt and pepper to taste
½ cup salted Spanish
   peanuts

Cook celery in a minimum amount of salted water for about 20 minutes. Drain and add the peanuts and white sauce. Season with salt and pepper.

PER RECIPE: 800 cal., 33 g. protein, 39 g. fat (10 sat., 24 poly.) FOR 4 SERVINGS, 200 calories per serving

ASPARAGUS PEANUT SCALLOP

1 pound fresh asparagus   2 tablespoons flour
½ cup chopped salted   1 cup skim milk
   peanuts   1 teaspoon salt
4 tablespoons oil   ½ cup bread crumbs

Cut asparagus into 1- to 2-inch lengths. Cook briefly in a minimum amount of salted water until nearly done. Drain. Arrange asparagus in shallow oiled casserole. Sprinkle peanuts on top. Prepare white sauce by combining 2 tablespoons of oil with flour, add milk and salt, and cook and stir until thick and bubbling. Pour white sauce over asparagus. Combine crumbs with remaining 2 tablespoons oil and sprinkle on top of white sauce. Bake in hot (400°) oven until crumbs are brown.

PER RECIPE: 1280 cal., 41 g. protein, 91 g. fat (12 sat., 38 poly.) FOR 4 SERVINGS, 320 calories per serving

SALADS

Our usual dinner salad is either leaf lettuce with an oil and vinegar dressing or a combination of lettuce, tomatoes, cucumbers, radishes, or green onions. This chapter, however, contains recipes for heartier salads which might well serve as a main luncheon or supper dish, or at least as a major part of the meal.

The winner of the bean salad popularity contest is, without doubt, Three-Bean Salad. Almost identical recipes have come to us from friends in several parts of the United States, some of whom use a sugar and vinegar dressing instead of the true French dressing given here (which we much prefer).

THREE-BEAN SALAD

1 (15½-oz.) can green beans

1 (15½-oz.) can wax beans

1 (15½-oz.) can kidney beans

1 cup thinly sliced celery

4 small green onions, sliced

2 tablespoons relish or chopped sweet pickle

½ cup vinegar-and-oil dressing

Salt to taste

Drain canned beans well. Mix with celery, onion, relish, and salt. Add salad dressing and marinate for several hours in the refrigerator before serving.

PER RECIPE: 1620 cal., 37 g. protein, 115 g. fat (16 sat., 66 poly.) FOR 8 SERVINGS, 200 calories per serving

KIDNEY BEAN SALAD

1 small onion
4 stalks celery
2 cups boiled kidney
   beans, or
1 no. 2 can kidney
   beans

¼ cup India relish
¼ cup boiled salad
   dressing
1 teaspoon salt
⅛ teaspoon pepper
Lettuce

Cut onion and celery into small pieces. Place in a bowl with cooked kidney beans. (If canned beans are used, pour hot water over them to remove sauce, then cool.) Mix India relish with boiled salad dressing, add salt and pepper, and mix with beans. Chill thoroughly and serve on lettuce.

PER RECIPE: 600 cal., 34 g. protein, 5 g. fat (1 sat., 1 poly.) FOR 4 SERVINGS, 150 calories per serving

HOT BEAN SALAD

This salad makes a good companion for cold ham or corned beef.

1 large stalk of celery
2 spring onions
1 (15½-oz.) can kidney
   beans
½ pound wax beans,
   cooked

Juice of ½ lemon
3 or 4 gratings of lemon
   peel
¼ cup mayonnaise
   diluted with ¼ cup
   skim milk

Slice celery and onions and mix with drained kidney beans and cut wax beans in a shallow oven-proof dish. Sprinkle them with lemon juice and add lemon peel. Dilute mayonnaise with milk, pour over bean mixture, and heat in oven until thoroughly hot, about 10 minutes in 350° oven.

PER RECIPE: 910 cal., 30 g. protein, 51 g. fat (8 sat., 25 poly.) FOR 4 SERVINGS, 230 calories per serving

WARSAW SALAD

This old recipe from Poland combines beets and crab meat with kidney beans. The original version probably did not contain crab but may have included fish when available, perhaps salted or pickled herring.

2 cups cooked drained
   kidney beans
2 cups cooked peas
2 cups cooked, diced
   beets
3 pickles, minced
1 (7½-oz.) can crab
   meat

3 onions, chopped
½ cup mayonnaise,
   diluted with ¼ cup
   skim milk
1 tablespoon prepared
   mustard
Salt and pepper to taste

Drain beans and peas well. Mix with beets, pickles, crab meat, and onion. Combine mayonnaise with milk and mustard and pour over the salad. Season with salt and pepper.

PER RECIPE: 1830 cal., 68 g. protein, 102 g. fat (17 sat., 50 poly.) FOR 8 SERVINGS, 230 calories per serving

FRANCES ANN'S BEAN SALAD

Kidney beans are used in salads in many combinations. This one features cabbage and hard-cooked eggs.

1 medium-sized green
   cabbage, shredded
2 cups drained, cooked
   kidney beans
¼ cup diced celery
3 pickles (dill or sweet),
   chopped

1 small onion, minced
¼ cup mayonnaise
Salt and pepper to taste
1 green pepper, chopped
1 tomato, cubed
2 hard-cooked eggs,
   sliced

Allow cabbage to stand in ice water for 10 minutes. Drain and set aside in refrigerator, where it will stay crisp. Combine all other ingredients except the egg and store in refrigerator. Just before serving, mix the cabbage with the other ingredients and garnish with sliced hard-cooked eggs.

PER RECIPE: 1820 cal., 57 g. protein, 112 g. fat (20 sat., 50 poly.) FOR 8 SERVINGS, 230 calories per serving

GREEN BEAN AND CUCUMBER SALAD

The combination of yogurt and cucumber gives a real freshness to this salad. Highly recommended for hot weather.

2 cups cooked cut green beans	½ cup yogurt
	¼ cup mayonnaise
1 medium-sized cucumber, sliced	Salt and pepper to taste
	1 teaspoon dill (optional)
6 green onions, cut fine	Lettuce leaves

Combine all ingredients. Cover and chill in refrigerator for several hours. Serve on lettuce leaves.

PER RECIPE: 600 cal., 9 g. protein, 53 g. fat (10 sat., 24 poly.) FOR 4 SERVINGS, 150 calories per serving

HOT GREEN BEAN SALAD

1 pound green beans	¼ cup cider vinegar mixed with ¼ cup water
1 slice bacon	
1 tablespoon oil	
1 teaspoon flour	Salt and pepper to taste
	1 small onion, minced

Cut the beans into 1-inch lengths and cook them in a minimum of salted water until just tender. Drain and place in serving dish. Meanwhile cut bacon into small bits; fry until crisp in a small skillet. Place bacon on absorbent paper to drain. Discard grease in skillet and replace it with oil. Rub flour into oil, add diluted vinegar, salt and pepper and cook, stirring constantly, until boiling. Pour it over the beans and sprinkle bacon bits and minced onion on top.

PER RECIPE: 330 cal., 11 g. protein, 19 g. fat (3 sat., 8 poly.) FOR 4 SERVINGS, 80 calories per serving

GREEN BEAN SALAD

The success of this salad is inversely proportional to the age of the beans. Our friend Carmella brings a version from Sicily in which tiny new potatoes, boiled in their jackets and then peeled, are added to the beans.

*1 pound young green
  beans
Pinch of fresh or dried
  basil
3 tablespoons olive oil
Juice of 1 lemon*

*Salt and pepper to taste
1 onion, minced
Trace of garlic juice or
  minced garlic
  (optional)*

Cook beans in minimum amount of salted water until barely tender. Drain and mix with basil, oil, and lemon juice. Chill. When ready to serve, season with salt and pepper, and mix with minced onion (and garlic, if used).

PER RECIPE: 580 cal., 10 g. protein, 43 g. fat (5 sat., 3 poly.) FOR 6 SERVINGS, 100 calories per serving

CHEF'S SALAD BOWL

This makes a good luncheon dish.

*½ onion
2 tomatoes
1 small head chicory
2 cups cooked peas*

*½ cup slivered, cooked,
  smoked or fresh beef
  tongue
¼ cup French dressing
Salt and pepper to taste*

Slice onion and separate into rings. Cut tomatoes into thin wedges. Break chicory into small sprays. Arrange attractively in a salad bowl with peas and tongue and pour the dressing over all ingredients; season with salt and pepper.

PER RECIPE: 790 cal., 32 g. protein, 47 g. fat (7 sat., 20 poly.) FOR 4 SERVINGS, 200 calories per serving

JELLIED VEGETABLE SALAD

5 sardines, chopped
1 cup cooked kidney
    beans
1 cup cooked peas
1 carrot, sliced or grated
1 stalk celery, sliced
1 apple, unpeeled,
    chopped

1 cauliflower, broken into
    flowerettes, cooked
    until almost tender
1 cucumber, sliced
4 tablespoons gelatin (4
    packages)
2 teaspoons salt
¼ cup lemon juice
¼ red cabbage, shredded
Lettuce leaves

Mix sardines and all vegetables except red cabbage. Dissolve gelatin in 1 cup boiling water, add 3 cups cold water, salt, and lemon juice. Allow to set partially, then mix with the vegetables in a bowl. Chill until set.

Scald red cabbage. Turn molded salad out on lettuce, garnish with red cabbage.

PER RECIPE: 850 cal., 32 g. protein, 7 g. fat (1 sat., 2 poly.) FOR 8 SERVINGS, 110 calories per serving

BEAN SPROUT SALAD

2 (1-pound) cans bean
    sprouts
2 tablespoons chopped
    green onion with tops
½ teaspoon sugar
1 tablespoon salad oil

1 tablespoon sesame
    seeds, browned and
    pulverized
3 tablespoons soy sauce
¼ clove garlic, minced
Dash cayenne pepper

Rinse the bean sprouts in cold water and drain well. Add the seasonings, mix thoroughly, chill, and serve very cold.

If you are lucky enough to obtain fresh bean sprouts, these should be washed well, then cooked for 2 minutes in boiling salted water, and drained thoroughly in a colander or wire basket.

PER RECIPE: 370 cal., 19 g. protein, 19 g. fat (2 sat., 9 poly.) FOR 8 SERVINGS, 50 calories per serving

CABBAGE-PEANUT SALAD

This is a combination we hadn't heard of until it was suggested by a friend and neighbor. We found the surprise of peanuts in the midst of the cabbage satisfying in both texture and flavor; altogether a delightful salad. For variety, add chopped apple and/or chunk pineapple. Some people prefer a sugar-vinegar dressing but we do not.

4 cups shredded cabbage
½ cup mayonnaise
2 tablespoons cider or, better, wine vinegar

¼ teaspoon monosodium glutamate
Dash pepper
1 cup salted Spanish peanuts

Chill cabbage. Blend mayonnaise, vinegar, monosodium glutamate, and pepper and chill. Just before serving mix the cabbage and dressing well, then stir in the peanuts.

PER RECIPE: 1790 cal., 44 g. protein, 160 g. fat (31 sat., 67 poly.) FOR 8 SERVINGS, 220 calories per serving

OLD-FASHIONED PEANUT-CABBAGE SALAD

Some people like a sweet-sour salad, and all the sugar does have the virtue that it keeps the cabbage crisp. But the cabbage will be beautifully crisp if it is merely soaked in cold water for 5 minutes and then refrigerated and the salad is eaten promptly after preparation.

2 tablespoons flour
Salt and pepper to taste
¾ cup sugar
2 eggs, beaten
½ cup vinegar, made up
   to 2 cups with water

3 tablespoons prepared
   mustard
1 large cabbage, shredded
   and chilled
½ cup roasted peanuts

Sift together flour, salt and pepper, and sugar. Combine eggs
with diluted vinegar and mustard. Add to dry mixture and
cook until thick, stirring continuously. Cool. Pour dressing over
cabbage, mix well, and stir in peanuts.

PER RECIPE: 1400 cal., 52 g. protein, 47 g. fat (11 sat., 11 poly.)
FOR 8 SERVINGS, 180 calories per serving

SICILIAN SEAFOOD AND VEGETABLE SALAD

On a hot summer day, put this together in the cool of the early
morning and keep it in the refrigerator. Serve it with seasame
crackers or hard rolls, iced tea or chilled dry white wine and
soda, and finish the meal with fresh fruit or fruit sherbet.

1 cup cooked or canned
   white beans
3 cups sliced boiled
   potatoes
1 (7¾-oz.) can tuna fish,
   drained and separated
   into bits
½ cup olive oil
2 tablespoons anchovy
   paste
1 teaspoon capers

3 tablespoons wine
   vinegar
1 tablespoon minced
   parsley
1 clove garlic, minced
Salt and pepper to taste
¼ teaspoon basil or a
   good-sized sprig of
   fresh basil
1 cup cooked shrimps
½ cup sliced Italian or
   Greek black olives

Put the beans, potatoes, and tuna fish in a bowl. Mix together
oil, anchovy paste, capers, vinegar, parsley, garlic, salt and pepper,
and basil. Pour half of this dressing over the ingredients in the

bowl and mix well. Arrange shrimps and olives on top and pour the rest of the dressing over all.

PER RECIPE: 2560 cal., 125 g. protein, 172 g. fat (23 sat., 18 poly.)

FOR 8 SERVINGS, 320 calories per serving

TOMATOES STUFFED WITH PEAS

Try this one *only* when you have tender, young, fresh peas.

8 tomatoes
3 tablespoons olive oil
1 tablespoon lemon juice

2 pounds fresh peas in the shell
½ cup mayonnaise
Salt to taste

Cut the tops from the tomatoes and scoop out the pulp (save it for another dish). Brush the insides of the tomato with a mixture of the oil and lemon juice. Shell the peas and combine them, uncooked, with mayonnaise and salt, fill the tomatoes, put the tops back on, and chill thoroughly.

PER RECIPE: 1580 cal., 20 g. protein, 141 g. fat (21 sat., 51 poly.)

FOR 8 SERVINGS, 200 calories per serving

GARBANZO SALAD

2 (15-oz.) cans
  garbanzos (chick-peas)
3 stalks celery, sliced
1 green pepper, chopped
1 onion, sliced and
  separated into rings

Salt and paprika to taste
¼ cup French dressing
  (vinegar-and-oil)
Lettuce leaves

Drain the garbanzos and rinse with cold water. Combine with the other ingredients and allow to marinate in the refrigerator for several hours before serving on lettuce leaves.

PER RECIPE: 1800 cal., 84 g. protein, 56 g. fat (10 sat., 32 poly.)

FOR 8 SERVINGS, 230 calories per serving

JAVANESE SALAD

This is good at any time of the year but it is best in hot weather.

1 cup salted peanuts
½ pound cooked, cleaned
  shrimps
2 cups shredded cabbage,
  crisped by soaking
  briefly in cold water
1 cup cooked green
  beans, in 1-inch pieces

1 cup scalded bean
  sprouts
3 green onions or
  shallots
1 large cucumber, sliced
  but not peeled

DRESSING:

¼ cup lime or lemon
  juice
1 tablespoon white sugar
1 tablespoon dark brown
  sugar

½ teaspoon salt
½ teaspoon paprika
1 tablespoon soy sauce

Combine all ingredients except cucumber with dressing. Chill thoroughly. When ready to serve, arrange sliced cucumber on top.

PER RECIPE: 1360 cal., 91 g. protein, 75 g. fat (16 sat., 21 poly.)
FOR 8 SERVINGS, 170 calories per serving

LENTIL SALAD

1 cup lentils
¼ cup French dressing
1 teaspoon salt

½ teaspoon freshly
  ground black pepper or
  to taste
Lettuce leaves

Soak and simmer lentils as described for beans in the introduction to the chapter on soups. Drain and add French dressing, season with salt and pepper, and allow to marinate in refrigerator for at least 1 hour. Serve on lettuce leaves.

PER RECIPE: 860 cal., 45 g. protein, 26 g. fat (4 sat., 13 poly.)
FOR 6 SERVINGS, 140 calories per serving

MOLDED LIMA BEAN SALAD

2 (3-oz.) packages
Italian-flavored or
lemon-flavored gelatin
1 tablespoon chopped
parsley
1 tablespoon chopped red
onion

1 (16-oz.) can baby
lima beans
1 (4-oz.) can mushrooms
3 apples
Lettuce
½ cup mayonnaise

Thoroughly dissolve gelatin in 1 cup boiling water; stir in 3 cups warm water. Add parsley and onion and chill until syrupy. Drain lima beans and mushrooms. Half-peel the apples; core and dice and combine with the limas and mushrooms in a mixing bowl. When gelatin is syrupy, combine with apples and vegetables in 2-quart mold and chill until set. Unmold on platter lined with lettuce. Serve with mayonnaise.

PER RECIPE: 2210 cal., 42 g. protein, 100 g. fat (17 sat., 50 poly.) FOR 8 SERVINGS, 280 calories per serving

LIMA BEAN SALAD

2 cups cooked lima
beans starting with
fresh, dried, or frozen
beans

¼ cup French dressing
Lettuce leaves
4 anchovy fillets, finely
chopped

Marinate beans in French dressing in refrigerator for several hours. Serve on lettuce leaves and top with chopped anchovy.

PER RECIPE: 710 cal., 24 g. protein, 42 g. fat (6 sat., 21 poly.) FOR 8 SERVINGS, 90 calories per serving

Or, instead of the anchovies, garnish the top of the marinated beans with 2 tablespoons grated onion and 1 tablespoon chopped parsley.

PER RECIPE: 640 cal., 17 g. protein, 38 g. fat (6 sat., 21 poly.) FOR 8 SERVINGS, 80 calories per serving

SOYBEANS

The soybean is famous for its nutritive value. It contains about 20 per cent fat and 30 to 50 per cent protein. This high protein content makes the soybean extremely valuable in areas where the diet is lacking in meat, fish, and dairy products. In vast areas of China and other countries of the Orient, the soybean has provided the main source of protein for many hundreds of years.

While we are all in favor of good nutrition, our interest in soybeans in this book is also concerned with the enjoyment of eating them. And in this regard plain soybeans have limited virtues; their real potential is brought out by various special processes, some very old, some very new. Among the newest soybean products are Textured Vegetable Protein. These are particularly useful where the intake of meat is restricted by reasons of health or religious beliefs, but we have been surprised to find they can be made into excellent dishes. These products are now available in beef-, ham-, and chicken-flavored as well as unflavored chunks and slivers suitable for soups, casseroles, and salads. Three recipes are given in this chapter but many more could be developed with a little experimentation. These products do not taste in the least like beans.

We have tried substituting soy for white or kidney beans in various recipes (a few examples are given below); while the end product was edible, we found the flavor and texture inferior to the white or kidney beans. Since the U. S. Department of Agriculture rates as "excellent" for use as vegetables some eighteen to twenty varieties of the two thousand distinct types now grown in the United States, further testing and tasting may produce better results.

To read of the many uses of soy products in adhesives, washable wallpaper, plywood glue, latex paints, inks, and so on, is not the best way to stimulate appetite. However, milk products have similar industrial uses and some by-products of the meat industry end up in unsavory applications. Soybean oil is put to excellent use in margarines, shortening, salad oils and dressings, and highly processed soybean flour is often an ingredient in sausages, pies, and bread. Soybean oil is much the most abundantly used oil in prepared commercial salad dressings. Soybean meal is the principal source of supplementary protein in feeds for livestock and poultry. The soybean has a rosy future "with its golden oil and its excellent protein, it represents a potentially most important source of food power for the entire world," in the words of our friend Dr. J. W. Hayward.

For many hundreds of years the Chinese and Japanese have eaten soybeans, most commonly as bean sprouts, bean curd, fermented bean pastes (miso), and soy sauce. Of these, bean sprouts are probably best known in this country, and while they can be produced by the germination of soybeans, mung beans are more commonly used.

Soybean curd, tofu, can be prepared in the home. Directions are given below if you care to experiment. The final product, which is whitish and has a soft delicate texture, is sold in slices or slabs, fresh or canned, and can be included in a variety of dishes. We think good fresh tofu is excellent and should be made more commonly available. It is widely fed to young children in China and Japan, giving them the benefit of its 6 to 17 per cent protein. Soybean curd is sometimes fermented with fungi to make soy cheeses which resemble the more highly flavored and odoriferous cheeses of Europe. The term applied to these in China is chou tofu which means "stinking bean curd."

Soy sauces, also called *soya, soja,* or *shoyu,* are produced in large quantities in China, Japan, and other countries of East Asia. They are made by a long and elaborate process of fermentation with various fungi, bacteria, and yeasts. Many kinds are prepared, different flavors being imparted by aromatic leaves, ginger, citronella, onions, fish, or chicken. When one of us was a small boy in the San Francisco Bay Area and already addicted to foreign cookery, soy sauce was available only in Chinatown. It was often called "beetle juice" by the white youngsters, who firmly believed it was made from black beetles.

A major part of the flavor effect of most soy sauce is contributed by its content of monosodium glutamate, but its flavor effect is not identical with that of Ajinomoto, Accent, MSG, or Enhance, all of which are useful but are simply pure crystalline monosodium glutamate. This material was first made available by a Japanese chemist who crystallized it from a crude soybean preparation. Currently, most monosodium glutamate in the United States is a by-product of beet-sugar refining.

According to the advertisements, monosodium glutamate "brings out the natural flavor of foods—adds no flavor of its own." This is not quite correct; monosodium glutamate is distinctly salty and has a flavor rather like a good beef broth. When added to meats, soups, and other foods, its taste effect is similar to that contributed by the addition of salted meat stock and superior to that from old-fashioned bouillon cubes.

Good soy sauce is made in the United States. We have been pleased to see Chun King soy sauce, made in Minnesota, all over the world, including Hong Kong. Another American soy sauce, sold under the La Choy label, also turns up abroad.

Soybean paste, *miso,* is very important in Japan, where it has been made for at least two thousand years; it is less extensively used in China. Its basis is cooked soybeans, yeast, and salt, and, sometimes, steamed rice; the mixture is allowed to ferment for two weeks or longer, up to several years. The rate of fermentation is controlled by the amount of salt added—the salt also serves to check the growth of undesirable microorganisms. Dark *miso* is made mostly of soybeans with only a small proportion of rice; white *miso* contains more rice and less salt. The product, which has a pastelike consistency, is usually made into soups, but it is also served with rice and other foods as a side dish or dressing. Many families use *miso* soup twice or even three times a day in a standard serving of about six ounces (150–200 cc.). In other words, *miso* soup in Japan is an item of most menus at any time of day, especially for breakfast. The *miso* stock is usually diluted by about eight parts of water to one of *miso*, with an average result, by analysis, that as it is consumed it is about 1.5 per cent sodium chloride. The Japanese housewife decides on the amount of water to use in the dilution by tasting for saltiness. Sometimes she adds more plain salt.

Traditionally the *miso* is prepared in the home once a year for use all year but an increasingly large proportion is made in factories. The ingredients—soybeans, salt (average of about 12 per cent), yeast, and water—are put in a wooden tub about sixteen inches in diameter and about thirty inches deep, with a wooden lid which fits loosely inside. This is weighted down by fifty pounds or more of stones.

Some of our Japanese colleagues think that *miso* soup is a major contributor to stroke, or "knock-down disease" as they call it in Japan, because of its high salt content. And it is a fact that the Japanese are probably the world's greatest salt eaters and have a very high incidence of brain hemorrhage. The incidence of stroke in Japan is highest where the salt intake is highest, and those regions show the biggest *miso* use, and also more cases of high blood pressure.

Soy milk is marketed in America both as a powdered milk and in the evaporated form. The demand for it is mostly from those allergic to animal milk. Soy flour and soy grits are also available for those with allergies, and can be used as cereals, in stews or soups or puddings, and in baked goods.

Soybeans are easy to grow in the home garden. They do well on all types of soil, but mellow or sandy loams are best. They can be planted any time from early spring to midsummer, and the green beans are harvested from mid-August to mid-October unless a severe frost occurs. The green soybeans must be shelled before they are served. When properly cooked they are still bright green and have a firm nutty texture. Recipes for their use are given below. They can be preserved by freezing or canning, while the mature beans are best preserved by drying.

I. DRIED SOYBEANS

TOFU

(SOYBEAN CURD)

Here are directions for the preparation of soybean curd at home, based on usual Chinese methods. This is a 2-step procedure: first the preparation of soybean milk, then the precipitation of the protein from the milk.

Soak 1 pound of soybeans overnight in 2 quarts of water in a cool place. Next day, discard the water, rinse the beans, then pour 2 quarts of boiling water over them, and blend, a portion at a time, in a blender for 2 minutes. Transfer to a large container and add 3½ quarts of boiling water, allow to stand for 10 minutes, stirring occasionally. Strain this through a triple layer of cheesecloth, saving the liquor, which should be brought slowly back to boiling and boiled for 1 minute. Cool to 185° and gradually stir into it ½ ounce of gypsum powder mixed in ½ cup of water. Continue to stir over medium heat; it will begin to curdle in 2 or 3 minutes, and the coagulation will be complete in less than 15 minutes. Remove the chunks of curd as they form, place them in a sieve lined with cheesecloth, fold the cheesecloth over the top, add a weighted plate (1½ to 2 pounds) and allow it to stand for 10 minutes. Remove the plate and cheesecloth and store the bean curd in water in the refrigerator.

There are two recipes for Bean Curd Soup in the soups recipe section.

BAKED SOYBEANS

1 cup dry soybeans (3
   cups cooked)
3 strips bacon
1 onion, sliced
½ cup tomato purée

½ teaspoon mustard
1 teaspoon salt
1 teaspoon chili powder
Pinch marjoram

Soak and simmer soybeans as directed for beans in the introduction to the chapter on soups. Cut bacon strips into small bits; fry out in skillet. Drain on paper, discarding drippings.

Drain beans and put in bean pot with all ingredients, adding boiling water to bring level of liquid to top of beans. Cover pot and bake in slow (250°) oven for 6 to 8 hours.

PER RECIPE: 940 cal., 83 g. protein, 52 g. fat (13 sat., 25 poly.) FOR 4 SERVINGS, 270 calories per serving

BRAISED PORK WITH BEAN CURD

Since bean curd is available in some cities in fresh and canned form in Chinese or Japanese groceries, a few recipes for its use are included.

2 bouillon cubes
½ teaspoon monosodium
   glutamate
2 pounds of lean pork,
   cut into 1-inch pieces
½ cup soy sauce
3 tablespoons sherry
3 cups onions, sliced
   lengthwise

⅓ cup shredded fresh
   ginger
2 cloves garlic, minced
2 tablespoons brown sugar
1 tablespoon cornstarch
2 (4"×1") cakes of bean
   curd

Make a stock of the bouillon cubes and monosodium glutamate in 3 cups of hot water. Place the pork pieces in a kettle, pour the stock over it, add the soy sauce, sherry, onion, ginger, garlic, and brown sugar, and bring to a boil. Simmer uncovered for about ½ hour or until pork is tender.

Simmer the bean curd in water for 20 minutes, drain and cut each cake into 3 pieces, and add to the pork mixture. Then add the cornstarch mixed with ¼ cup of cold water. Simmer until smooth and thickened, stirring constantly.

PER RECIPE: 2550 cal., 230 g. protein, 130 g. fat (42 sat., 24 poly.) FOR 8 SERVINGS, 320 calories per serving

SOYBEANS IN TOMATO SAUCE

1 pound dry soybeans
½ pound lean pork
1 onion, chopped
1 green pepper, chopped

3 (6-oz.) cans tomato sauce
2 tablespoons chili powder or to taste
Salt to taste

Soak the soybeans overnight in 3 quarts of water. In the morning drain and put them to cook in 2 quarts of fresh water, bring to a boil, and simmer for 1½ to 2 hours. Cube pork and add it to the beans with the onion and green pepper. Simmer for 2 hours. Turn into bean pot, add tomato sauce, chili powder, and salt and cover. Bake at 250° for 2 hours or longer.

PER RECIPE: 2360 cal., 236 g. protein, 116 g. fat (16 sat., 17 poly.)
FOR 8 SERVINGS, 300 calories per serving

SOYBEAN LOAF

2 cups cooked, mashed soybeans combined with liquid
1 cup fine bread crumbs
1 egg
½ cup evaporated milk

1 onion, diced
1 tablespoon oil
1 tablespoon minced parsley
Salt and white pepper to taste

Sauté onion in oil. Combine all ingredients and turn into oiled loaf pan. Bake at 350° until nicely browned.

PER RECIPE: 1170 cal., 70 g. protein, 43 g. fat (11 sat., 15 poly.)
FOR 4 SERVINGS, 290 calories per serving

II. GREEN SOYBEANS

Green soybeans must be shelled before they are served. This is best done by pouring boiling water over them and allowing them to stand for 5 minutes. Then drain and cool. Break the pods crosswise and squeeze out the beans, which are then ready to cook.

Cook 2 cups of shelled beans in 1 cup of water with ¾ teaspoon salt in a covered saucepan for 15 to 20 minutes. The beans will not soften as peas do, but will retain their firm texture. They are now ready to be used in one of the following recipes.

CREAMED SHRIMPS AND SOYBEANS

1 *cup shrimps, cooked
and cleaned*
2 *hard-cooked eggs,
chopped*

1 *cup cooked green
soybeans*
1 *cup medium white
sauce*

Combine ingredients and heat thoroughly. Serve on toast.

PER RECIPE: 1000 cal., 81 g. protein, 54 g. fat (9 sat., 23 poly.) FOR 6 SERVINGS, 170 calories per serving

GREEN SOYBEAN AND VEGETABLE SALAD

1 *cup cooked green
soybeans*
1 *cup sliced celery*
2 *raw carrots, chopped*

2 *tomatoes, diced*
½ *cup oil-and-vinegar
dressing*
Lettuce

Mix soybeans, celery, carrots, and tomatoes with dressing. Chill and serve on lettuce leaves.

PER RECIPE: 1050 cal., 30 g. protein, 84 g. fat (8 sat., 44 poly.) FOR 8 SERVINGS, 130 calories per serving

SOYBEAN AND CARROT RING

4 cups grated raw
carrots
1 cup bread crumbs
4 eggs
2 teaspoons salt

4 tablespoons oil
1 cup skim milk
2 cups cooked green
soybeans

Mix carrots with bread crumbs. Beat eggs and add salt, oil, and milk. Add this mixture to carrot-and-crumb combination. Pour into an oiled ring mold, set in a pan of hot water, and bake in a slow (325°) oven until firm. Before serving, fill center with hot, cooked green soybeans.

PER RECIPE: 2060 cal., 100 g. protein, 109 g. fat (18 sat., 47 poly.)
FOR 8 SERVINGS, 260 calories per serving

GREEN SOYBEAN TOMATO ASPIC

1 tablespoon gelatin
2 cups bouillon
1 cup tomato juice
1 tablespoon lemon juice

½ cup chopped celery
1 cup cooked green
soybeans

Soak gelatin in ¼ cup cold water and dissolve in hot bouillon. Add tomato and lemon juices and chill until mixture begins to thicken. Add celery and green soybeans, pour into mold, and chill until firm.

PER RECIPE: 460 cal., 43 g. protein, 14 g. fat (3 sat., 8 poly.)
FOR 6 SERVINGS, 80 calories per serving

III. SOY FLOUR

WHOLE WHEAT-RYE BREAD WITH SOY FLOUR

1 cake yeast
¼ cup brown sugar
1 tablespoon salt

1 cup soy flour
1¼ cup whole wheat or
    graham flour
3 cups medium rye flour

Crumble yeast into 2 cups lukewarm water. After 5 minutes add brown sugar, salt, and 1 cup of whole wheat flour, then stir in soy flour sifted together with rye flour. Mix well. The dough will be quite soft. Allow it to rise at room temperature for about 2 hours, or until doubled in bulk. Sprinkle remaining ¼ cup whole wheat flour on board, turn bread out and knead briefly, then divide into 2 parts and put in oiled bread pans. Cover with oiled wax paper and a clean towel. Allow to rise until bread is even with the tops of the pans. Bake at 350° for 1 hour. Makes 2 loaves.

PER RECIPE: 1820 cal., 71 g. protein, 20 g. fat (2 sat., 8 poly.)

ITALIAN BREAD WITH SOY FLOUR

1 cake yeast
6½ cups unbleached
    white flour

1 tablespoon salt
½ cup soy flour

Soak crumbled yeast cake in 1 cup lukewarm water for 5 minutes, add 2 cups lukewarm water, 2 cups flour, and salt. Stir well and leave to rise on kitchen counter for ½ hour. Sift soy flour together with 1 cup flour and add it to the bread. Then add the rest of the flour, stir in as much as possible, then turn bread out on floured board and knead until smooth and well mixed. Oil bowl, and return bread to it; cover with a plate or oiled wax paper and a clean towel and allow it to rise at room temperature for 1 hour, or until doubled in bulk. Turn out again on floured board, knead briefly, then shape into loaves. This will make 3 "French" loaves. Allow to rise another ½ hour, then brush crust with water and bake in 350° oven ½ hour.

PER RECIPE: 2760 cal., 91 g. protein, 15 g. fat (1 sat., 4 poly.)

IV. A NEW SOY PRODUCT

HAM À LA KING MADE WITH TEXTURED VEGETABLE PROTEIN

½ pound Textured Vegetable Protein ham chunks, hydrated
2 green peppers, chopped
1 pimento, chopped

1 hard-cooked egg, chopped
1 cup medium white sauce
4 slices toast

Combine ham chunks, green peppers, pimento, and egg with white sauce and heat in the top of a double boiler. Serve on toast.

PER RECIPE: 1500 cal., 139 g. protein, 40 g. fat (6 sat., 14 poly.)
FOR 4 SERVINGS, 380 calories per serving

TEXTURED VEGETABLE PROTEIN CHICKEN SALAD

¾ pound Textured Vegetable Protein, chicken-flavored granule, hydrated
2 hard-cooked eggs
1 cup finely chopped celery

12 stuffed olives, chopped
½ cup mayonnaise
Salt and white pepper to taste
Lettuce

Mix all ingredients well and chill. Serve on lettuce.

PER RECIPE: 2240 cal., 183 g. protein, 120 g. fat (21 sat., 49 poly.)
FOR 6 SERVINGS, 370 calories per serving

BEAN COOKERY IN
IMPERIAL ROME—APICIUS

The popular picture of society in ancient Rome is one of hedonistic luxury—of rich people lolling in the baths, watching great spectacles, and feasting elaborately. After two thousand years Lucullus is remembered more for his extravagant banquets than for the military exploits that brought the wealth that paid for the banquets. But in all the ruinously expensive competition to seek out rare foods and prepare complicated dishes in the most exotic manner, the Romans lacked some items basic in modern cookery, especially those foodstuffs brought to Europe from America more than a thousand years after the last of the Roman emperors.

The Romans used honey as a sweetener—sugar was unknown. They had nothing like potatoes or tomatoes, and the nearest approach to the common bean (*Phaseolus vulgaris*) was the broad bean (*Vicia faba*). But peas, lentils, and chick-peas (*Cicer arietinum*) were cultivated and eaten by rich and poor alike. Recipes were given by Apicius in the world's oldest surviving book on cookery. Apicius lived in the first century and it seems that he wrote a book of general recipes and a work on sauces, but all that remains is a rewrite by an unknown editor sometime around the year A.D. 400. This is preserved in two manuscripts, dating from the ninth century, one now in the Vatican Library in Rome, the other in the Library of the New York Academy of Medicine.

Apicius' book, first printed in Latin in 1498, has been re-printed, re-edited, and translated many times. In English, it is available in translation by J. D. Vehling (1936, *Apicius: Cooking and Dining in Imperial Rome*, W. M. Hill, Chicago), and by B. Flower and E. Rosenbaum (1958, *The Roman Cookery Book: A Critical Translation of the Art of Cooking by Apicius*, George G. Harrap, London). Vehling's translation contains errors and bold interpretations but has the advantage of being made by a professional cook. Flower and Rosenbaum experimented with cooking some of the recipes and gave explanatory notes. Paolo Buzzi's modern Italian translation (1957, *Apicio: La Cucina di Roma*, Veronelli Ed., Milan) is good. Buzzi's rendition lacks index and provides very few explanatory notes, but many of the food items, implements, and procedures seem less strange in Italian than in English.

Apicius apparently wrote for the experienced cook: he seldom specified quantities or cooking details. The ingenuity of the cook was required by such instructions as this for a dish made with dried peas, leeks, herbs, and spices: "If something is lacking, add it and serve" (Book V, iii).

One ingredient frequently used by the Romans, *liquamen* in Latin, defies translation. Vehling seemed to think it was any kind of court bouillon or herb-flavored broth and so specified it in his English translation. Paolo Buzzi dodged the issue and simply translated *liquamen* as *"salsa d'Apicio"* (Apicio's sauce) in his Italian edition. Acutally, *liquamen* in the days of the Romans was a product made from fish and salt, commercially available from factories. The entrails of fish were salted and sun-dried for several months, frequently shaken or stirred with a stick. When thoroughly dried, the mixture was sifted and was, as far as we can make out, in the form of a salty powder. A liquid version was also made by boiling fish in brine.

Though nothing like *liquamen* has come down through European cookery, the Chinese *ho yow*, or oyster sauce, seems to be similar. This is made by salting and drying oysters and is used on various meats and also in dishes made with legumes. The Chinese insist that this is not interchangeable with soy sauce. Apicius' recipes do not mention salt where *liquamen* is listed as an ingredient so some salty preparation, perhaps fish-flavored, should be used for these.

Practically every recipe of Apicius calls for herbs or spices, usually both, but the list is not long and tends to be repeated over and over; presumably flavor was varied by using different proportions. It may be that the few herbs specified by Apicius were his favorites or, more likely, only those few were generally available and used, even as the Italians today use a smaller variety of spices and herbs than we do in the United States. Because Apicius gives few details of the actual cooking and seldom says anything about quantities, it is not possible to guarantee that the modern cook can truly duplicate his Roman dishes. But after nearly two thousand years we can still be grateful to Apicius for some additions to our recipe files.

In the sample recipes below, we have taken liberties in interpretation in order to provide recipes and instructions suitable for the modern kitchen and food supplies in the United States. While Apicius gave recipes for both beans and peas, it must be remembered that the beans we now use were unknown to the Romans until after the discovery of the Americas. In our effort to reproduce the ancient flavors and textures we have done most of our experimenting with dried peas, which should resemble the peas of imperial Rome more closely than the American bean resembles the *fava* bean. Three of the examples are given with literal translation from the Latin.

I. THREE RECIPES WITH TRANSLATION AND INTERPRETATION

PISAM FRIGIDAM

TRANSLATION:
Cook the peas, stir, and chill. When they are cold, stir again. Mince onion and the whites of hard-boiled eggs, and season with oil and salt. Add a little vinegar. In the serving dish, garnish with the egg yolks which have been passed through a strainer, pour green oil over all, and serve.

COLD PEAS

INTERPRETATION:

Perhaps we might call this dish a salad—a cold purée of cooked dried peas mixed with onion, seasoned with French dressing, and garnished with hard-cooked egg.

Soak and simmer dried peas; allow to cook to a thick purée, stir, and chill. Mince whites of hard-cooked eggs and spring onions, and stir into the peas with oil and salt. Add a little vinegar, heap on lettuce leaves on a serving plate, garnish with the yolks of hard-cooked eggs put through a sieve, pour a little olive oil* over all, and serve.

PISAM INDICAM

TRANSLATION:

Cook the peas. When they have been skimmed, cut up leeks and coriander, add to the kettle, and boil. Take small squids with their ink and cook them this way. Add oil, *liquamen*, wine, and a bouquet of leeks and coriander. Allow to cook. When done, pound together pepper, lovage, oregano, and a little caraway; moisten with liquid from the pan, diluted with wine and raisin wine. Cut the squid into small pieces, add to the peas (with the sauce). Sprinkle with pepper and serve.

DRIED PEAS, INDIAN STYLE

INTERPRETATION:

Soak dried peas. Add chopped leeks and chopped fresh corian- der (if this is not available, substitute parsley) and simmer for 1 to 2 hours. Meanwhile cook small squids in their own ink with a bouquet of leeks and coriander or parsley, oil, soy sauce, and wine. When they are done, cut the squids into small pieces and add to the peas. Grind together pepper, marjoram, celery seed, and a little caraway (and coriander seeds, if fresh corian-

* The Latin and Italian versions clearly specify "green" oil. Green olive oil is still served in some farm homes in Italy where they press their own oil. In The Marches in central Italy we were fortunate enough to feast on fresh, fresh finocchi (fennel) at its very best served with green oil and a little salt. The oil has a lovely pale green color, is quite thick, and has a delicate flavor.

der was not used), moisten with the cooking liquid from the squids diluted with wine and raisin wine. Add this to the peas and squids, reheat, and sprinkle with freshly ground pepper before serving.

LENTICULA

TRANSLATION:

Take a clean pot*, put in the lentils, and cook them. Put in a mortar and pound some pepper, cumin, coriander seeds, mint, rue, pennyroyal. Moisten with vinegar, add some honey, *liquamen*, and boiled must. Mix all with the vinegar, then pour into the pot. Mince the boiled mussels, add, and bring to a boil. When boiling well, allow to reduce. Add green oil in the serving dish.

LENTILS WITH MUSSELS OR CLAMS

INTERPRETATION:

Put lentils to soak in a kettle with ample water; after several hours bring to a boil, reduce heat to simmer.

Combine freshly ground black pepper with ground cumin and coriander seeds, a minced mint leaf, and pinch of thyme; moisten with vinegar, add honey, soy sauce and wine, or grape juice, which has been condensed by boiling, then add to lentils. When lentils are done, mince and add boiled mussels or canned minced clams, cook and stir lentils until liquid is reduced, or thicken with a paste of flour and water. Transfer to heated serving dish and pour a little olive oil over the lentil-mussel mixture.

* Apicius' directions frequently call for a "clean" or even a "new" pan or pot, and this can be taken quite literally to mean a new pot. The kind of pottery used for cooking was coarse and was not glazed, and would have been difficult to clean even with modern detergents and scouring devices. It was, at the same time, very cheap, and apparently was thrown away as readily as we discard the aluminum containers in which our TV dinners and other frozen foods are packaged, to be cooked in once and then thrown out.

II. FURTHER INTERPRETATIONS OF APICIUS' RECIPES

GREEN BEANS

The fresh beans known to the Romans were not the string, snap, or pole beans to which we are accustomed in America, but were *fava* or broad beans, much coarser and more fibrous distant cousins. Apicius gives these suggestions for cooking them.

I. Cook the beans with soy sauce, oil, fresh coriander or parsley, cumin seeds, and chopped leeks.

II. Fry the boiled beans; serve them with soy sauce.

III. Boil the beans and serve them with mustard, honey, pine nuts, cumin seeds, and vinegar.

IV. Boil the beans, then chop finely. Serve with fresh celery, leeks or shallots, oil, soy sauce, and a little boiled wine or grape juice.

FRESH SHELLED BEANS

I. Boil the beans and serve with salt, cumin seeds, oil, and a little wine.

II. Boil the beans, then fry them, and season with soy sauce and freshly ground black pepper.

III. Cook the beans with fresh fennel; season with pepper, soy sauce, and a little boiled wine or grape juice.

IV. Boil the beans and serve them without seasoning except salt.

CONCHICLA OF PLAIN PEAS

The word *conchicla* probably refers to a shell-shaped serving dish or mold. We suggest scallop shells or individual oven-proof dishes.

Soak and simmer dried peas with a bouquet of leeks and parsley. When the peas have cooked to the consistency of thick porridge, add freshly ground black pepper, oregano, soy sauce, and a little wine. Place the mixture in oiled shells, top with oiled bread crumbs, and bake in moderate oven until the crumbs are brown.

CONCHICLA À LA COMMODUS

Soak and simmer dried peas. Season them with freshly ground black pepper, dill, marjoram, and dried onion flakes. Add soy sauce and a little wine. Mix well, then add 4 eggs to each pint of peas, place in a mold, set the mold in a pan of water, and bake in a 350° oven until set, about ½ hour.

CONCHICLA WITH CHICKEN

While this recipe calls for dried peas, it asks for peas that remain whole when cooked. For this reason we suggest chick-peas for a more interesting result.

Cut a frying chicken into small pieces. Simmer in a mixture of wine, oil, and soy sauce. When tender, take it out of the sauce and remove the bones. Put the chicken in a casserole, add the sauce in which it was cooked, chopped onion and parsley, cooked chick-peas, freshly ground black pepper, and cumin seeds. Cook over a low fire or in a slow oven until thoroughly hot.

III. RECIPE TESTING, ALMOST TWO THOUSAND YEARS LATER

The two recipes below were worked out by experimenting with different quantities of the ingredients and seasonings in the preceding recipes, and the versions given here are those we like best. Apicius gave no indication of the way these dishes should be served. We cooked the dried peas to the consistency of mashed potatoes and served them as a vegetable. Consistency contrast can be provided by the addition of slivered almonds, thinly sliced raw celery or shallots, sliced water chestnuts or bamboo shoots, or other crunchy garnish. Or spread in a shallow casserole, cover the top with oiled bread crumbs, and place under the broiler until the crumbs are brown.

ROMAN-AMERICAN SPLIT PEAS

1 cup split peas
3 green onions with
    tops, sliced
1 stalk celery, sliced
½ teaspoon ground
    coriander

⅛ teaspoon pepper
½ teaspoon celery seed
⅛ teaspoon basil
2 teaspoons soy sauce
¼ cup dry white wine

Bring the peas to a boil in 3 cups of water, cover, and allow to stand for an hour. Add all other ingredients, bring to a boil again, then simmer for an hour or longer, until the peas are done to the desired consistency. Instead of simmering on direct heat, the peas can be cooked in a bean pot or casserole with a cover in a slow (250°) oven.

PER RECIPE: 740 cal., 49 g. protein, 2 g. fat (trace sat., 1 poly.) FOR 4 SERVINGS, 190 calories per serving

PEAS OR BEANS IN THE STYLE OF EMPEROR VITELLIUS (A.D. 69)

This sweet-sour version of dried peas is a good accompaniment for ham or other smoked meat or highly seasoned sausage.

1 cup split peas
⅛ teaspoon pepper
1 teaspoon salt
½ teaspoon celery seed
2 tablespoons olive oil

¼ cup flour or two eggs
    for binding
¼ teaspoon ginger
¼ cup sweet wine
¼ cup honey
¼ cup wine vinegar

Bring peas to boiling in 3 cups of water. Cover and allow to stand for an hour. Bring again to a boil, add honey, wine, vinegar, salt, pepper, ginger, and celery seed, and simmer on low heat for an hour or longer. Thicken by adding 2 eggs mixed with ¼ cup cold water or flour made into a paste with ¼ cup of water; add to the peas and stir as you continue to cook until thickened. Stir in the oil and taste for seasoning; following Apicius' advice, "If something is lacking, add it and serve."

PER RECIPE: 1340 cal., 52 g. protein, 30 g. fat (5 sat., 3 poly.) FOR 6 SERVINGS, 220 calories per serving

INDEX